The Journey Behind the Adventure

✈ ✈ ✈

Dr. Daney Dumdeang

Published by Franklin Publishers

Printed in the United States of America

For permissions, inquiries, or additional copies, contact:

Franklin Publishers

www.franklinpublishers.com

Acknowledgements

The author would like to thank and express his gratitude to Mr. Thong-in for his help in making this important book in the desired time. Everyone should be aware of his sincere hardship in making this book.

Thank you

Dr. Danny

Introduction

Introduction of the author's journey and mission locally and throughout the globe.

First of all, the author thanks Tom, who highly inspired me to write on this topic, the topics of my traveling both locally and worldwide. We both discussed this topic or subject matter that we should write about or reorganize my traveling experiences to those interested in traveling. Most of my missions are both voluntary and assigned by the US government.

Some books of my journey have been privately published in both biographies, first and second volumes, but not in a better writing fashion and writing style and easy for readers. We should have published it independently as one book II itself; maybe my writing in my personal mission journey, as well as governmental duties, will help the traveler writers and readers interested in travelers and the experiences of my journey. I have spread out everything you need to know to start a career as a working travel writer from scratch. I have observed many different writers and researchers for academic degrees. Those are different writers and editors describe the verity aspects of travel writing as a live hood using real samples from their own experiences and careers, so my writing style is as my own experiences, to share with readers both adventurers excited experience in multiple cultures, languages, food, social behaviors, and the likes.

This book provides you the answers to the most common and important questions new travel writers have. It covers them in perfect detail and, in many cases, using step-by-step examples, the processes that every travel writer should go through to maximize their chance of success.

Hopefully, you readers of this book will be enjoyable and hopefully for you who have some interested in worldwide traveling with both the author and my assistant.

Good luck.

Sincerely,

Dr. Daney Dumdeang

Thankful Note

The author would like to profoundly give special thanks to the venerable Luang Poo Siri Dharma Khan of Wat Arun Rajvaram, who encouraged me to write this traveling subject when he visited me in the USA and I took him, showing him around Northwestern regions, including Canada. We both enjoyed every moment of our time being together. Even though he is no longer with us, his spirit will happily receive that I have done his request, likewise.

My dear friend, whom my assistant has always carefully requested me to write on this essential subject... here is the book that has been published and is available in the book marketplace.

The author dedicated his hard work to both of them, Luang Poo Phrakru Siri Dhamma Khan and Tom Rodpradit.

Thanks to all who kindly supported.

Sincerely

Dr. Daney Dumdeang

President, Dumdeang Foundation

My intention in publishing this book is to contribute to everyone who joined the creation of the new life of Nong Ubon Dumdeang

I intend to print this book to give to everyone who comes to celebrate the new life of Nong Ubon Damdeang.

Thank you Note:

The author thanks and thanks Khun Thong-Intr Rodpradit, who has assisted in getting this crucial book done in no time. One should recognize his sincere work hard on this book.

Thanks

Dr.Daney.

Note

All funds raised from the sale of this book will be used to support and care for the dogs and cats that Nong Ubon raises on her farm, which she loves like her own family, and to provide health care for them as if she were a veterinarian examining them herself.

Thank you for your kind donation and support.

Dr. Sompong Danny Damdaeng

Table of Contents

Author's Biography
Dr. Sompong Danny Dumdeang

In his youth, the author was first ordained as a novice monk at Wat Phang Tri, where he studied the Khmer language, astrology, palmistry, fortune-telling, Abhidhamma chanting, the Mahachat sermon, Phra Malai scripture, and Buddhist traditions for one year.

Later, he pursued Pali grammar and the Dhammapada at Wat Sam Bo before continuing his studies in Dhamma and Pali, eventually attaining the highest level of Nak Tham (Dhamma scholar). He later became a novice monk with Pariyatti (scriptural) qualifications at Wat Hua Pom in Songkhla Province. Following this, he advanced his studies in higher-level Pali at Mahachulalongkornrajavidyalaya University, a leading institution for Buddhist education under the Thai Sangha, while residing at Wat Mai Piren in Thonburi, Thailand.

While studying at Mahachulalongkornrajavidyalaya University, the author was elected as the president of the student body. His key responsibilities included fundraising efforts to support the university. Additionally, he was appointed as the chief editor of the university's magazine, *Siang Dhamma* (*Voice of Dhamma*).

Today, the university offers bachelor's, master's, and doctoral degree programs in various disciplines for both monastic and lay students.

The author graduated from the Faculty of Southeast Asian Studies at Mahachulalongkornrajavidyalaya University (which was later renamed the Faculty of Humanitarian Studies). In 1983, the university administration decided to divide the Faculty of Humanitarian Studies into two separate faculties: the Faculty of Humanities and the Faculty of Social Sciences.

The author was entrusted with responsibilities by the former Acting Supreme Patriarch, who served as the Chairman of the Acting Supreme Patriarch Council.

Somdet Phra Phutthachan "Kiew Uppaseno" of Wat Saket Ratchaworamahawihan in Bangkok, during his tenure as Rector of the Buddhist University, appointed the author as the leader of the first group of Dhammaduta (Buddhist missionaries). The author was assigned to train and teach laypeople, monks, and novices in the northern provinces, particularly establishing a base of operations at Khao Kho, Phetchabun Province.

His teachings focused on Thai language education, psychological aspects of religion and culture, behavioral guidance, and hygiene. He also taught hair-cutting skills as part of a United Nations program. Additionally, the author played a key role in bringing many hill tribe youths to ordain as novice monks and fully ordained monks at Wat Benchamabophit in Bangkok.

The author had a deep interest in the way of life of all hill tribe groups, but he was particularly fascinated by the language of the Hmong people. He diligently studied and recorded Hmong vocabulary daily. Eventually, the Department of Public Welfare under the Ministry of Interior published his compiled vocabulary as a reference resource.

Later, when the Hmong migrated to settle in the United States, the author played a key role in assisting them in accessing education and building a better life. He did this through the Ministry of Education's service area under the English as a Second Language (ESL) program.

Additionally, he dedicated more than a decade to advocating for the legal rights of hill tribe people, Asian immigrants, and even American citizens. The author also taught Dhamma at the headquarters of Wat Mahathat and at an elderly care home.

In Bangkok's Bang Khae district, the author also taught Dhamma at an elderly care home and served as a Dhamma lecturer on the *Dhamma for the People* radio program broadcast by the Territorial Defense Department.

Later, he pursued further studies in India for two years, specializing in archaeology at Banaras Hindu University. He was then awarded a Fulbright scholarship to study in the United States, where both Harvard University and the University of Washington offered him admission. He ultimately chose to continue his education at the University of Washington.

Throughout his career, the author was invited to lecture at prestigious universities across the United States and around the world. He also served as a professor at various universities.

The author is the founder and president of two companies: International Cleaning Services, Inc. and American Asian International Contractor. These companies were established to assist Indochinese refugees fleeing the Vietnam War and arriving in the United States. The author also provided support to immigrants from all over the world.

As a result of these efforts, the companies received the prestigious Outstanding Performance award. They achieved great success in their operations, which led to the companies being recognized as Federal Partners, a status granted by former U.S. President George H. W. Bush.

After the Vietnam War ended, a massive wave of refugees from Vietnam, Cambodia, Laos, and other countries sought employment and settled in the United States. These refugees required assistance from the U.S. government, particularly in areas such as education, social integration, and healthcare.

One of the key requirements for healthcare was the ability to communicate effectively. As a result, the author was appointed as an official interpreter at various hospitals, with authorization granted by the U.S. Supreme Court.

The author was honored by the U.S. Supreme Court and appointed as an associate judge. His primary responsibility was to participate in the adjudication of cases concerning crime and social issues.

The author has worked as a lawyer, establishing a law firm to assist disadvantaged individuals. He also served as a cultural liaison between Americans and people from various countries around the world.

The author has played an important role in activities related to Buddhism, culture, and national security, both in the East and the West, starting from the time of Princess Phuunphitmay Ditsakul. By incorporating Buddhist principles and beliefs, he has trained and taught millions of people, inspiring them to live purposeful lives, leading to a good and happy life on this Earth.

The author has been recognized as an outstanding individual (WHO IS WHO) by People Magazine in America. He was honored for his work as a sociologist, a media representative, the editor of the Asian Report newspaper, and a true advocate of democracy. The author has deeply studied and understood both Western and Eastern philosophy.

The author has had a long-lasting love for pets. Once, he was deeply shocked and saddened by the passing of two beloved pets: a dog named Bubu, a purebred poodle, and a cat named Sammy. Currently, the author has pets that are part of the family, including a dog named Rama, an Australian Shepherd, and two turtles named Tata and Tutu. The magazine *Animal Pet Companion* once described him as a person who loves animals with a heart and soul that is rare to find.

When not teaching law or engaging in philosophical debates on politics, economics, and society, the author finds happiness in cooking and gardening. He also spends part of his time traveling around the world whenever the opportunity arises. The author once had the chance to take his wife, Patty, an American, to meet with...

The author had the honor of meeting the Pope in Rome, Italy, in 2004. He was also granted the privilege of engaging in a philosophical discussion on Buddhism and Christianity with His Holiness.

The author established the Dumdeang Foundation, a charitable organization under U.S. law, where they serve both as the founder and executive president. The foundation's headquarters is located at 1138 S.E. Reynold Street, Portland, Oregon 97202, USA. During the opening ceremony of a Thai temple in America, Phra Phrom Mangkhalajarn (also known as Phra Phanya Nanta) praised the author in front of the Thai community in America and Americans, calling Dr. Sompong Dumdeang a close disciple. He also highlighted the author's pioneering efforts in founding the foundation in the U.S. to help disadvantaged individuals.

The Dumdeang Foundation played a significant role in supporting society. For example, in December 2004, when the tsunami occurred in Thailand, the foundation partnered with the U.S. government to provide aid to the victims of the disaster. Additionally, the foundation helped establish hospitals and clinics to assist disadvantaged individuals in Sri Lanka and India in collaboration with the governments of both countries.

Even though the author has lived in the United States for over 50 years, they have always maintained a deep love and connection with their homeland. Whenever possible, the author travels back to visit Thailand, taking the opportunity to visit relatives who mostly reside in the provinces of Songkhla and Satun.

On one of their trips, the author wished to return to visit Kho Kho, an area that was once a restricted zone for the public in 1968. This area was associated with communist insurgents aiming to separate the land. The author has a deep interest in this historical site.

At that time, the author was appointed by the Thai clergy to be the first Buddhist missionary to assist the hill tribes in spreading religious teachings and helping them to cooperate with the government. As a result of this mission, the author received a scholarship from the British Columbia University in Canada to conduct research on the hill tribes in Thailand.

The author studied Arabic and Persian at Washington University for about three years, collaborating with Dr. Nicholas from the Department of Middle Eastern Studies. Together, they conducted research and developed a comparison of Buddhist philosophy, specifically the concept of Nirvana and the Sufism school of thought in Islam. Both the author and Dr. Nicholas observed that both Nirvana in Buddhism and Sufism in Islam are integrated phenomena, merging philosophy and politics within both religions. The focus is on truth, which must be relevant to human life. This perspective suggests that conflicts or contradictions will not arise at the level of Sufism. Therefore, the author attempts to present a worldview to Muslims, emphasizing that our world has transcended conflicts, ethnic divisions, and injustices.

The author is a volunteer and a member of the Office for Emergency Management, an organization under the U.S. government known as FEMA (Federal Emergency Management Agency). It was established during the presidency of Jimmy Carter. FEMA's primary responsibility is to coordinate efforts to address natural disasters and emergencies that occur in various locations across the United States.

The author feels deeply proud of their contribution to society by personally donating funds to build hospitals and elderly care homes in India and establishing clinics in Sri Lanka. They were also the head of the Northwest Medical Team, which assisted tsunami victims in Asia in 2004. In December 2005, they returned to reflect on the event and to donate clothing, medicines, and educational funds from the Red Cross Foundation, as well as funds from the Good Samaritan religious organization, to Thailand, Indonesia, India, and Sri Lanka.

The author is a well-known author whose works have been acknowledged by readers in the fields of philosophy and Buddhism. They have written numerous articles on history, society, and religion as well.

1. **Buddhist Philosophy**: The thesis was written to obtain a doctorate degree and was submitted to the Graduate School of the University of British Columbia in Canada.

2. 2. 21st Century BUDDHISM

3. Article on Buddhist Monks and Hill Tribes: Titled *Buddhist Monk and Mountainous People*, this article was written in 1980 (B.E. 2523) as a study material for students at the University of Washington.

4. Guide to the Constitution of Life: Published in Thailand in 2005 (B.E. 2548).

5. Crisis...Conflict 3: The Southern Border Provinces: Co-written with Intrakiet Rodpradit, with the author as the primary writer.

เบื้องหลังการผจญภัยจากการเดินทางท่องเที่ยว

The Journey behind Adventure

✈ ✈ ✈

Chapter 1

The benefits of traveling

Travel, whether near or far, domestically or abroad, always has its benefits. Every time we travel, even though we may get tired or spend all our money, trust me, we always gain something in return. So, what exactly do we gain from traveling around the world? Today, we'll share stories from travelers about what they've gained from their journeys.

New experiences

The phrase "new experiences" is always an important concept that we gain after traveling. Many people might wonder why these experiences are so significant. Imagine that we are like a blank piece of paper. Traveling can be compared to adding colors to that paper, making it vibrant and beautiful. New experiences will give us more stories in life. At the very least, they become memories that we can share with our children and grandchildren for many years to come.

Making new friends

Traveling the world not only allows us to see new places but also gives us the opportunity to meet new people. Meeting new people helps us exchange experiences with each other. New friends don't necessarily have to be of the same age—they could be older or younger. In the places we visit, we might gain new perspectives or ideas from them. Who knows, some of these people could even become important companions in the future. It's always better to make connections.

New ideas.

For people who work and need to use their thinking or require inspiration and new ideas, traveling around the world is incredibly important. Traveling exposes you to new experiences, perspectives, and environments that can spark creativity, provide fresh ideas, and motivate you. It's a great way to break away from routine, recharge your mind, and gain insights that can be applied in work or personal life.

Being in a new environment and encountering various experiences will always spark new ideas. When we combine these new encounters with our previous experiences, we can create something new. For those who feel stuck or lack creative ideas, trying this method could help. It may lead to fresh and innovative ideas.

Reflect on oneself

For those who are feeling bored, stressed, or unable to find a way out, we recommend taking some time for solitude and traveling alone. Even just a short trip, like 2 days and 1 night, can be very beneficial. Traveling alone allows us to reflect on ourselves, sit down and look at the problems we've faced, find solutions on our own, and also get some rest. This can be very helpful. Perhaps, for those who are currently confused or uncertain about something, traveling alone around the world might help them make some important decisions.

Fulfilling one's duties within a set timeframe is considered a good practice. However, if we become too strict with work and life, it can feel like being bound by ropes too tightly, which may break sooner than expected. It is best to relax and take some time to travel. This will help bring more happiness into life.

Chapter 2

The Author and Travel

Travel is an important part of life. The author has had the opportunity to travel and visit various places almost all around the world. The author has recorded memories related to these places that they have visited and experienced, which are valuable experiences. Therefore, the author would like to share these experiences with all readers.

The first time traveling abroad was to compete in an international sports competition between Thailand and Malaysia.

In 1954, the writer studied in the junior high school at WachirAnukul School, Mueang District, Songkhla Province, where Teacher Adul Dulayaphan was the headmaster. The writer earned the trust of Teacher Adul, who assigned them as the team leader for the group of Boy Scouts and Girl Guides to represent Thailand. The group traveled to participate in a conference aimed at fostering friendship among Scouts and Guides in Malaysia and Singapore.

The writer always remembers that Teacher Adul had great faith in them. He told the writer that they were a strong student and a Scout with high responsibility, suitable to be the leader of the Boy Scouts and Girl Guides in their group during the trip to the conference.

Sompong... you are a strong and highly enthusiastic child. You have the potential to bring fame to our school and our country without much difficulty. However, you must learn to be less stubborn and reduce your defiance. Listen to your superiors from time to time—this will be the path to your great success in the future. You will shine brightly like a star among all the others. Sompong... remember this. I care about you, and that's why I am advising you. But the only thing that would disappoint me about you is your stubbornness.

We... The four Scouts and Girl Guides, consisting of three girls and one boy (the writer), set out on a journey by bicycle from Hat Yai. Our destination was Malaysia and Singapore, covering a distance of over 700 kilometers.

Before our departure, our school held a grand farewell ceremony in our honor. Scout songs were sung at intervals as a mark of respect for us as representatives of Thailand and as a tribute to King Rama VI, who had established the Scout movement in Thailand.

The resounding voices of Scout songs echoed along our cycling route, gradually fading as we rode farther and farther away. Eventually, we could no longer hear the songs at all.

Scout Salute Song

I, a Scout of Thai blood, bow with respect,
Humbly honoring the royal feet of our revered King.
His Majesty King Rama VI, our guiding light,
With boundless grace, founded and nurtured the Scouts.

He tirelessly trained and shaped our ways,
Instilling love for nation and faith in our hearts.
He taught us skills, wisdom, and deeds,
A shining beacon of Buddhist virtue and strength.

Like the radiant moon and the sun's bright rays,
Illuminating the world with wisdom and grace.
His kindness shall forever remain,
Deep in our hearts, unwavering and true.

Song of the Vajiravudh Scouts

The Vajiravudh, the royal crown, protector of the people,
Brought forth the Scout movement, and I humbly follow in its path.
We, the Scouts, of Thai descent,
Honor and uphold the King's glory with loyalty.

We, the Scouts, reflect on his kindness,
And pledge our allegiance to the King, our nation, and religion.
Let us rise as Scouts, to do good,
For the honor and dignity of the Thai Scouts, as it is our heart's desire.

At that time, even though the four of us were exhausted from the long journey on bicycles, our spirits were filled with joy and pride for the opportunity to serve our country as representatives in the sports competition in Singapore and Malaysia. As the team leader and the only male participant, I always treated the three female students with the utmost respect. There was no sense of gender difference whatsoever. We all embarked on the journey with peace of mind, hopeful for victory and the chance to bring home trophies to present to our school, Songkhla province, and our nation. However, what I will explain is that nothing in this world is certain, as the events that unfolded with us proved.

While riding our bicycles along the railroad tracks heading towards Georgetown and Penang Island near the Perang River, the train sped by at high speed, and we were caught off guard. Terrified to the extreme and driven by survival instinct, the three girls jumped into the river. Although I was shocked, I managed to keep my composure. The first thing I did was to help the three girls who had fallen into the water survive and escape the grasp of death. I decided to jump in and assist them. Perhaps it was due to some miraculous force that guided my actions

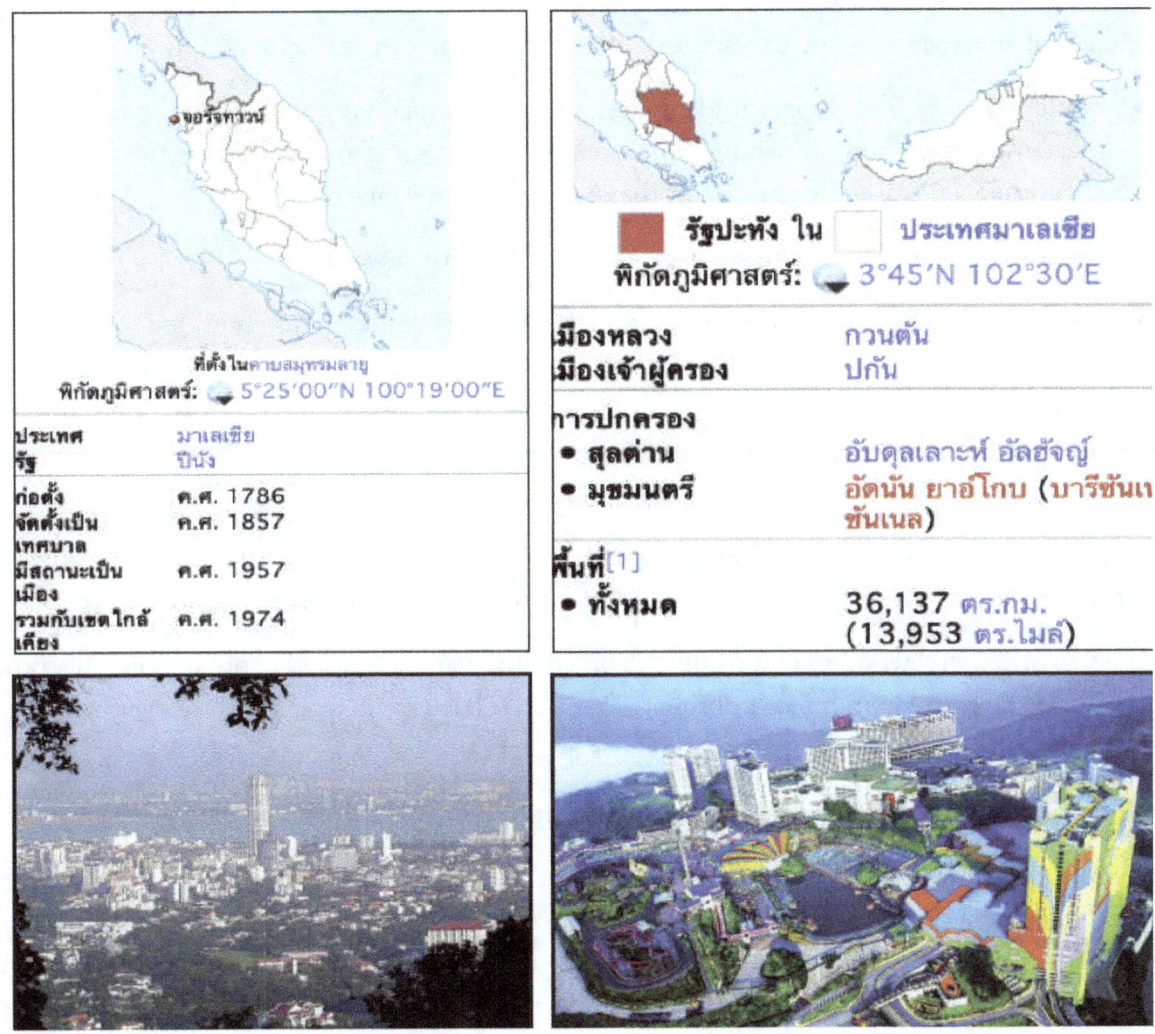

(Left) Georgetown City (Right) Perang City, Malaysia.

It was a miracle that they were saved by God's grace. I managed to help all of them to safety, except for one girl who was in worse condition than the others because she couldn't swim. I had to get her to hold onto my back and carry her to the shore. I still don't know how I was able to help her in that critical moment, but it was a feeling of great pride. As a high school student at that time, I had helped a fellow student who was traveling with us to compete in the sports event to survive the drowning incident. It was an event that felt like a miracle, one I will never forget in my life.

A local newspaper in Penang reported the incident, which garnered widespread attention from the people of Penang. We were deeply moved by their kindness, which we could never forget. They saw that our bicycles were damaged and, as a result, gave us enough money to buy new bicycles for everyone. The incident was also reported to the authorities on Penang Island.

Next, we traveled by car to the office of the governor of Penang. The governor provided us with great assistance. The people of Penang were also very kind and helpful. Many questions arose, such as, 'Who are we? Why did they help us so willingly?'

They are good citizens, Muslims who have faith in Allah. A good person, no matter their ethnicity or religion, will always feel a sense of responsibility toward humanity in the same way.

We would like to express our gratitude to everyone who helped save the lives of the three girls from Hat Yai, preventing them from drowning. We were honored by the people of Georgetown, who praised us as brave children and wished us success in the competition in Malaysia.

The great success, receiving the prestigious 'Golden Wolf' award.

We spent a total of 8 days traveling nearly a thousand kilometers to Ipoh and Kuala Lumpur, the capital city of Malaysia, to participate in the international sports competition between Thailand and Malaysia. During that competition, the team from Thailand won and was recognized as the most courageous sports team, the 'Tiger Cubs' team.

I also received a prestigious award as the brave person who saved the lives of the three girls from my team, helping them survive the drowning incident. That was the 'Golden Wolf' award, the highest honor from the Global Tiger Organization, in line with the principles of other members and the nation.

Upon returning home, we were warmly welcomed. The Vajiryanukool School in Songkhla province organized a grand reception in honor of bringing happiness back to them. They were overjoyed to see us return home with victory instead of receiving news of death.

We received a grand and prestigious welcome from Songkhla province.

A grand and prestigious reception was organized for us, with the governor presiding over the ceremony. This was a significant event that had never occurred before in the history of our school. I was honored and praised as a courageous person, a youth who should be looked up to as an example for helping to save the lives of my fellow travelers without regard for myself and without fear of the risks to my life.

The governor once said something very meaningful: 'The fact that the writer helped his fellow travelers survive the drowning incident is something admirable and should be an example for others. Whether in times of war or any other situation, we must stand together, whether alive or dead. This is a good example. We should live together without prejudice to race, nationality, or religion, as student Sompong Dumdeang has done, and he is the best role model for our community.'

Additionally, the governor praised the three girls as good role models for the community and society and thanked their parents for being good examples to the community. What was most surprising was when the governor asked the writer, Sompong Dumdeang, what he had to say.

The writer felt deeply moved and overwhelmed, unable to speak. Only tears flowed down the face. The writer's tears at that moment were tears of joy and pride, and also tears of sorrow for the incident that occurred with the three girls who traveled together at that time.

Chapter 3

Visit the South of Siam, the beautiful border

The writer was born in Non-District, Songkhla Province, Thailand. Later, the family migrated and settled in Khuan Kha Long, Satun Province. Although the writer has lived in the United States for more than 60 years, they have never forgotten their hometown. Whenever the opportunity arises, the writer will bring their family back to visit relatives in Thailand.

The writer has visited and interacted with the indigenous people of the Orang Asli or Sakai tribe in various mountainous areas across several provinces in southern Thailand. This was during the time before they traveled abroad to study, marking the beginning of the writer's journey.

Since the writer had a deep interest in the traditional way of life, existence, and culture of the Orang Asli or Sakai tribe for a long time, coupled with the fact that the writer chose to study archaeology at the graduate level at Banaras Hindu University in India, this led to a continuous fascination with studying ancient history and archaeology. Therefore, the writer wishes to present knowledge regarding the ancient human tribe called the Orang Asli or Sakai, as follows:

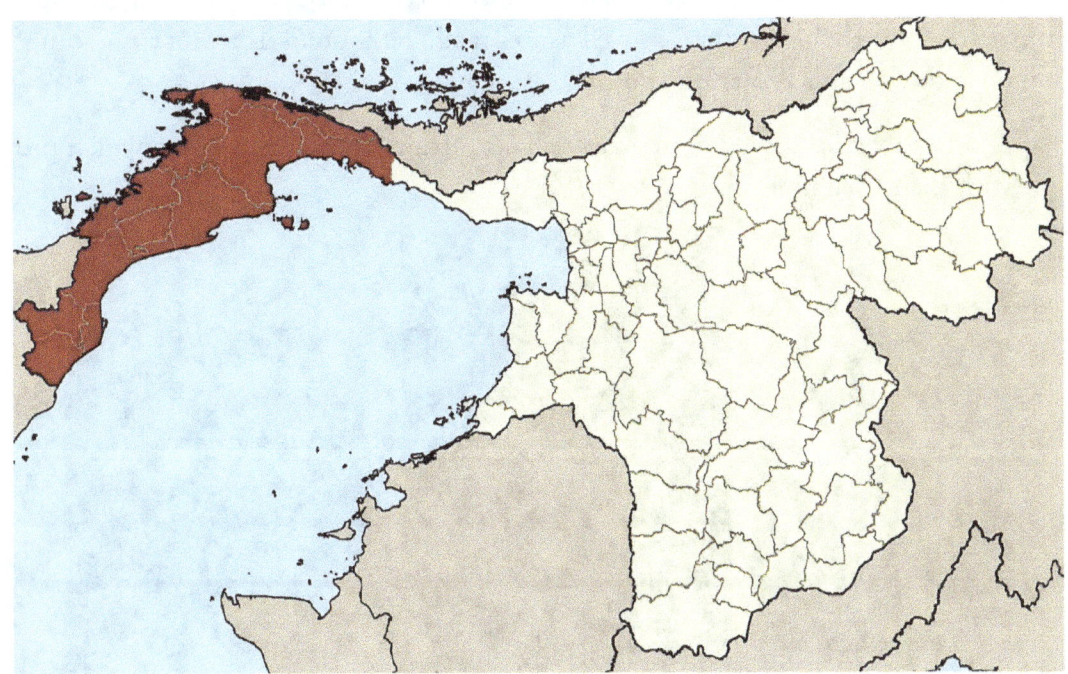

The Sakai are an ancient human group that has existed since the Stone Age, approximately 15,000 to 150,000 years ago, or even longer. They have a slim physique, dark skin, thick lips, and a flat nose. Their height is generally short, and they have frizzy hair that does not grow long. They belong to the Australoid race, similar to the Aboriginal people of Australia. They live in small groups of around 7 to 60 individuals, mainly found in the state of Kedah in Malaysia, the interior of Papua Island in Indonesia, the Philippines, and the Andaman Islands in India. They refer to themselves as "Mani," while others call them Orang Asli, Orang Asli Sakai, or simply "wild men" (Sakai).

There has been a hypothesis regarding the origins of this group of people, suggesting that they might have migrated from Africa before the modern Homo sapiens. Their characteristics are similar to those of the indigenous people of Papua New Guinea and the Aboriginal people of Australia. Research in Australia has indicated that the Aboriginal people diverged into a distinct group long ago, with archaeological evidence in Australia dating back more than 60,000 years. If this hypothesis is true, it would mean that these populations have been living in both Asia and Australia for at least 100,000 years.

It is believed that over the past several thousand years, there has likely been intermingling with the Austroasiatic ethnic group (which is Mongoloid) that migrated down from southern China around 3,000 to 5,000 years ago, giving rise to the current Mon-Khmer ethnic group.

In foreign countries, such as Malaysia, this ethnic group is referred to as the "Semang." In 2002, a population survey found around 2,000-3,000 individuals, and currently, it is estimated to be around 4,500-5,000 people.

The Ngao Pa or Sakai people in Thailand

The Ngao Pa, or Sakai, in Thailand are an indigenous tribe or prehistoric humans who lived along the borders of Nakhon Si Thammarat, the Sangkala Kiri Mountains, and the Phu Kerd Mountains. These three mountain ranges form the backbone of the southern region of Thailand. This group of people has long been the dominant population for over 100 years, before evidence suggests that the local population lived around Krabi province, as well as in Trang, Nakhon Si Thammarat, Satun, Songkhla, Yala, Pattani, Narathiwat, and Phatthalung provinces.

In the past, they lived in fertile forest areas rich with fruits and wild animals, which provided the Sakai people with their livelihood.

 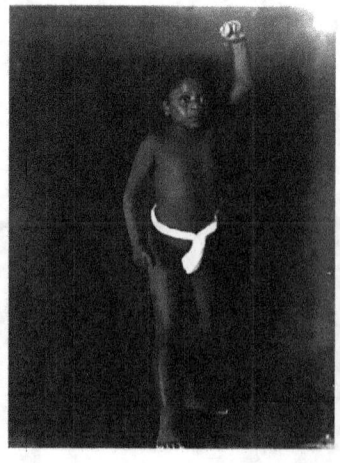 

Kanang Kiratoka

The wild man who received a high rank from King Chulalongkorn (Rama V)

They are comfortable. These people will form a group and travel, wandering across various provinces such as Trang, Pattalung, Satun, and Songkhla. They ventured into Yala and crossed the border into Malaysia. When the forests were destroyed, the abundance of resources significantly decreased. The indigenous people had no place to live, so most of them migrated to Malaysia, where the forest remained abundant. They became urban dwellers, settling in government-designated areas, primarily in Than To district, Yala province. Nowadays, they have adapted to urban life, wearing clothes, having TVs, and using fans.

The wild man received Royal Kindness from King Chulalongkorn (Rama V), who graciously appointed him as a special royal servant.

Phon Serepao, Kanang Kiratka, was a wild man who became well-known after receiving care from King Chulalongkorn (Rama V). The King graciously allowed him to stay in the Grand Palace to serve as a special royal attendant. According to records, Kanang shared stories of the way of life of the Sakai people with the King, which inspired the King to write the play "The Wild Man," in which Kanang was made the main character.

Once, King Chulalongkorn (Rama V) traveled to Nakhon Si Thammarat. The town presented a wild man from Phatthalung for the King to observe. After viewing the man, the King became interested in the wild people and had the idea to raise one for himself. He ordered his attendants to find a wild man but not one who was too young—someone manageable but not too young, and insisted that the child be an orphan without parents.

The news reached "Ngoh Yang," the leader of the wild people in Phatthalung. He informed the King that there were two orphans in his group: Kin and Kanang. Ngoh Yang proposed that a "menorah" performance be arranged to entertain the wild people until they fell asleep, after which the King could select one of them.

The wild child who was carried out while asleep became the inspiration for the character in the play "Ngoh Pa" (The Wild Man), where the main character was often depicted with red flowers adorning his ears.

Although Kanang came from a marginalized wild tribe, often considered primitive, he proved himself to be an intelligent and sharp child with an excellent memory. Initially, when he first entered the palace, his diet consisted mainly of cooked rice and bananas with water, but over time, Her Majesty the Queen encouraged him to try other foods. When presented with unfamiliar dishes, he would ask the names to show respect to the food. Normally, Kanang did not wear clothes, regardless of whether it was hot or cold, but later, he was made to wear clothing. Once he started wearing clothes, he added numerous

9

accessories, including ceremonial outfits and formal attire, all designed by King Chulalongkorn (Rama V).In the royal palace, Kanang lived a comfortable life with caretakers who ensured his hygiene, but he was still unfamiliar with many aspects of palace life. In particular, when it came to using a toilet, he initially used a pot, and after finishing, he refused to wash his hands or use paper towels, only wiping them with wood.

When Kanang became a royal servant, he worked diligently in response to the king's orders. Whenever King Chulalongkorn (Rama V) woke up, Kanang would quickly dress beautifully to attend to him. During meals with the royal family, Kanang would sit close to the king, who would often ask about various matters, such as the well-being of the wild people in Phatthalung. One of the king's regular questions was, "What do you eat with rice in the morning?" He also asked Kanang to teach him the words of the wild people for the royal writings. In addition to his duties, Kanang had a talent for acting. Although it was difficult, he was able to perform well. When the king wrote the play "The Wild Man," with Kanang as the main character and had Mom Bunnak as his instructor, Kanang performed excellently and accurately despite having little time to practice.

In December 1905 (B.E. 2448), King Chulalongkorn (Rama V) ordered a photograph of Kanang to be printed and sold for 3 baht per sheet, which was considered expensive at the time. However, the photographs did not sell well, and only 230 copies were printed. As a result, more prints were made, and they eventually sold for a total of 1,200 baht. The proceeds were divided into three parts: the first part was donated to the temple, the second covered the cost of paper and ink for printing, and the third portion was given to Kanang as an allowance for his expenses.

After the reign of King Chulalongkorn (Rama V), the next monarch, King Vajiravudh (Rama VI), took Kanang into royal service. He was appointed as a forest ranger in the Royal Forest Department, responsible for the king's protection and also served in the Royal Household Department. On March 23, 1914 (B.E. 2457), King Vajiravudh bestowed upon him the name "Kiratoka."

Disappeared

The story of Kanang from then on is mostly unknown, as no one had much information about him. One year after the passing of King Chulalongkorn (Rama V), Kanang went to live with the royal bodyguards and then disappeared. Even though King Vajiravudh (Rama VI) ordered multiple searches to find him, no one was able to locate Kanang. His disappearance from Thai history is considered a great loss, as no one has seen him again.

Chapter 4

The longest journey
After coming to live in America

Since the writer came to live in America as a student, they completed their Ph.D. at the University of Washington. Their peers, who also graduated with a Ph.D., choose different paths. Some became teachers (internships), while others became researchers. The writer, who graduated with great honors, they were appointed as instructors in a new position specifically created for them. The writer was honored to be the first person at the University of Washington, which is one of the top ten universities in the United States.

After completing their studies at the end of 1971, trusted students such as Richard, Jef, and John purchased a new minivan and planned to travel for educational exploration and to experience new environments. They set off from Seattle, heading toward New York, marking the farthest trip the writer had taken since arriving in the United States in 1960. Initially, the writer planned to invite Patty to join the trip but was concerned that it might not be convenient for her, as all the students were male. The long road trip in a van seemed more suitable for men, so she was not included. However, she was supportive and encouraged the writer despite not being part of the journey.

We started our journey on the evening of August 19, 1971, from Seattle, Washington. We traveled on Highway 84 north, heading steadily until we reached Appleton, then continued to Tri-Cities and onward to Spokane, passing through Ohio. We stopped to visit the monument of President Roosevelt and the battlefield of General Custer. Even though the writer was a teacher, they were still in their youthful years.

Together with the three students, we enjoyed ourselves to the fullest. We didn't feel tired, even though the journey was tough. We drove steadily along the highway without resting. There was nothing but youthful joy and excitement. We took turns driving and occasionally stopped to refuel and buy food, drinks, and beer to enjoy in the car. The writer slept in the car before reaching the city of Madison, La Crosse, in the state of Wisconsin.

The long-distance journey along the highway from Seattle to New York was a lengthy car trip. We drove both directly and detoured depending on the points of interest we wanted to visit. For example, to see General Custer's battlefield, we had to take a detour to the town of North Dakota, among other places.

To avoid feeling lonely, we would stop to drink beer and smoke marijuana, creating a youthful, carefree atmosphere. However, as a teacher, the writer drank in moderation, and everything went smoothly. After driving for a long time and feeling tired, Jeff took over the driving responsibilities.

An accident occurred in Wisconsin. Jeff was driving, and at that moment, the writer was asleep in the car. After Jeff had been driving for a long time and was exhausted, the writer was suddenly jolted awake by a loud noise. The writer was thrown out of the sleeping area and violently collided with the refrigerator inside the van. This impact caused the 11th and 12th ribs to break, and the writer lost consciousness immediately after the vehicle hit a power pole with great force. The accident took place in a field, far from the town of La Crosse, and occurred in the middle of the night, so there was no lighting on the road. It took over an hour for the ambulance to arrive.

The writer felt great suffering. The emergency ambulance took them to Francis Hospital in La Crosse on the night of August 24, 1971. The writer received excellent care from the emergency room doctors and nurses, with one nurse named Linda taking special care. She showed deep concern and attention, and when she learned from the students that the writer was their professor, she became more interested in the writer. She had an interest in Buddhism even before meeting the writer, and they often discussed topics like good karma and bad karma. However, she didn't know the meaning of the words "karma" and "kama" (which means sex). One time, during their conversation, she said, "Let's have karma tonight," which made the students laugh. She was confused and asked why they were laughing and was shocked when she learned the meaning of "karma" related to sex. She apologized for the mistake and later sent a letter to the writer, explaining that she now understood the meaning of "kama" and had intentionally used the word as an expression of love toward the writer (sexual expression).

When the writer returned home to Seattle, they continued to receive letters from Linda. To avoid any misunderstanding or false hope, the writer replied, explaining that they already had a partner, which was why Linda hadn't joined the trip. It was a "man's trip," and they had agreed on that. Linda responded, saying she would wait until the writer broke up with their partner, which the writer found a bit unrealistic. Over time, the writer stopped replying to her letters, and eventually, they lost contact.

Deceived

In the Francis Hospital, where the writer stayed for 11 days, several events occurred. The doctors and nurses provided treatment using strong medications, including painkillers, which caused the writer to become disoriented and lose consciousness. During this time, an insurance company representative pretended to be helpful and offered assistance, stating that the insurance would cover the entire hospital bill. At that moment, the writer was under the influence of medication (on drugs), which impaired the mind and caused confusion. The representative held the writer's hand and had them sign a consent form agreeing to only pay for the hospital expenses. The writer, lacking awareness at the time, signed the consent form. The document stated that the insurance company would not be responsible for covering injuries, damages, or lost work time. The writer was unable to understand the full rights and benefits at that moment. Later, the writer realized they had been tricked into signing the consent form. This was a painful experience, as the American automobile insurance company engaged in fraudulent practices, leaving the victim to suffer from the consequences of the events that occurred.

The writer thanks God for helping them recognize deceit and fraud through indirect means. This became an inspiration for the writer to help other disadvantaged people who are at a disadvantage or have fewer opportunities. After the writer's condition improved, they called their elder brother in Singapore to inform him about the accident. They also called a student named Easter to inform her and called Patty to let her know that the writer had been in a car accident.

As for the nurse named Linda, who took care of the writer after the writer left the hospital, she knew that the writer, being Thai, would likely want to visit the Thai Pavilion exhibition in Wisconsin. Therefore, she sent an invitation letter. However, the writer did not respond to the invitation.

There is one observation: It is common for female nurses to often fall in love with doctors or for doctors to fall in love with female nurses, though the latter happens less frequently.

In cases where doctors or nurses fall in love with their patients, it is quite rare. However, in the case of the nurse who took care of the writer, it is an unusual situation. She became fond of the writer, who was a university professor, possibly because of her deep interest in Buddhist philosophy. When she met the writer, who was teaching Buddhist philosophy, this likely influenced her feelings. However, when the writer informed her that he had a partner, and after returning home from the hospital and not responding to her letters, communication between them ceased.

After being discharged from the hospital and fully recovering, the writer arranged to purchase a new van since the previous one was too damaged to continue using. The writer, along with three students, traveled to New York City to teach meditation to people of all ages and backgrounds, including both young and elderly individuals. Most of the attendees were business leaders interested in the training.

The meditation teachings received an excellent response due to the growing interest in Eastern philosophy and meditation in the West at the time. This led to the program's success. Afterward, the writer traveled to Southampton, England, at the invitation of a businessperson to teach meditation to a group of wealthy individuals, including property owners and yacht owners. The two-week training was well-received.

After completing the course, the writer returned to Seattle, Washington, where they underwent a health check-up at a hospital and was declared in good health.

The writer's domestic travel within the United States on this occasion was incredibly valuable and filled with unforgettable experiences. The writer received praise from the General of the United States Army, General [name not provided].

General John Newland and General Gordon were both close friends of General Thanom Kittikachorn during the Korean War. They were very close, and both praised the writer. This was due to the social situation in the United States during the 1960s, where the children of the wealthy or the offspring of the ruling class often rebelled, refusing to go to school and instead lived carefree lives. However, the children of both generals were devoted to learning. They admired the writer for teaching Eastern philosophy, and they were the writer's students at Washington University, majoring in philosophy and religion. They were eager to learn about meditation and had a deep interest in Eastern culture, which made them rare and exceptional students.

General Newland spoke about his fellow comrade-in-arms from Thailand, Field Marshal Thanom Kittikachorn, saying that he came from a poor country, but his heart was greater than any mountain. He also served as the Prime Minister of Thailand for over 10 years.

Chapter 5

The author and the return to visit Khao Kho

The memorial to the martyrs is built in the shape of a triangle using soft stone. The size and shape of this memorial hold significant meaning. The triangular shape symbolizes the collaboration between civilians, police, and military personnel. The base is 11 meters wide, representing the year 1968, which marked the beginning of intense operations against communist insurgents. The height from the platform to the top is 24 meters, representing the year 1981, which saw the start of a major military operation. The height from the foundation to the top is 25 meters, symbolizing 1982, the year the combat operations ended. Each side of the triangular base measures 2.6 meters, representing the year 1983, when the construction of the memorial began.

In the battlefield of Khok, part of the operation involved the Chinese Hmong troops of the 93rd Division (Gok Min Tang), who were stationed at Doi Mae Salong in Chiang Rai. They sent their forces to assist in suppressing the communist insurgents in the Khok area. Their mission included guarding and constructing the road from Thung Samo to Khok.

Currently, Khok has undergone significant development and transformation. Once a region of insurgency, it has become a beautiful natural tourist destination in Phetchabun Province. Each year, millions of tourists visit Khok to enjoy its scenic beauty. This is because Khok is a stunning mountain area with cool weather all year round.

The author and the co-author, in their capacity as editors of several books written by the author, have been collaborating and consulting on the production plans for various books, such as *The Life, Work, and Mission of Dr. Sompong Damdaeng and His Family* (Volumes One and Two), *Crisis... The Conflict in the Three Southern Border Provinces*, and *MARLEY: Loyal and Modern Dog*. These discussions took place at the Imperial Resort and Hotel's restaurant in Khok, Phetchabun Province.

It has been over 50 years since the author had the opportunity to visit Khok again, as intended. After leaving the so-called "Red Zone," which at that time was a restricted area, the author entered a region known as the stronghold of insurgents seeking to establish communist ideology in Thailand. There were clashes with government forces. In 1965, the Communist Party of Thailand, abbreviated as CPT, began infiltrating the Khok area and Phu Hin Rong Kla, expanding their influence to the population who felt they were treated unjustly by the government, as well as to various ethnic groups.

14

The day the gunfire began

In the beginning, the Communist Party of Thailand relied on certain ethnic hill tribes, particularly the Hmong, as key figures in expanding their base through propaganda, emphasizing the lack of care and justice provided by the government. They coordinated with student leaders in cities who felt they had been treated unjustly and opposed the authoritarian rule of the time. This led to training with weapons and strategic planning in a systematic manner, supported by foreign countries governed by communist systems. In 1965, the Communist Party of Thailand began their operations in Phetchabun Province. On November 20, 1968, the insurgent group in Khok declared "The Day the Gunshot Was Heard" by attacking the village of Lao Luea. Many government officials were wounded and killed, and the Communist Party seized some weapons. They spread propaganda, claiming that the authorities would retaliate with a purge, killing everyone in the village. This caused the villagers to fear and hate the authorities, leading many to flee and join the insurgents.

Since then, Khok became the starting point for the government's efforts to suppress the insurgents, covering the districts of Chon Daen in Phetchabun Province, Nern Maprang, and parts of Nakhon Thai District in Phitsanulok Province. The battles between the insurgents and government forces during this time caused significant damage, resulting in the loss of lives among soldiers, police, and civilians. The violence created widespread fear, and there seemed to be no sign that it would end easily.

The author was the leader of the first missionary group of Thai monks.

The Thai monkhood recognized the dangers posed by insurgent ideologies, which threatened the safety and property of the people in the area, especially the hill tribes. As a result, they decided to establish the first missionary group to send monks to teach Buddhism to the hill tribes and to provide a means for them to leave the insurgent groups. This initiative not only allowed the spread of Buddhism among the hill tribes but also helped ease the burden on the government. However, the monkhood insisted that only senior monks, with at least five years of ordination, should be chosen to teach the hill tribes to ensure the effectiveness of the mission.

The author's name was proposed to be the leader of the first missionary group. However, there were issues and obstacles, as the selection committee initially rejected the author due to the fact that the author had fewer than five years of ordination. Ultimately, a suitable monk with the necessary qualifications and knowledge to spread Buddhism in the Khok area could not be found. The committee then reconsidered the author's qualifications, which met all the criteria of the monkhood, except for the ordination period. As a result, they presented the case to His Holiness Phra Phromkhunaphon, who was responsible for overseeing the selection of missionary monks, requesting an exemption from the ordination period requirement for the author.

At that time, His Holiness Phra Phromkhunaphon was the Rector of Mahachulalongkornrajavidyalaya University and also one of the author's teachers. Believing in the author's abilities, he agreed with the selection committee's decision. (His Holiness Phra Phromkhunaphon was the abbot of Wat Saket and was later appointed as Somdet Phra Phuttha Chan, serving as the acting Supreme Patriarch until his passing.)

The author thus became the representative of the Thai Sangha, serving as the head of the first missionary delegation to carry out religious duties in the insurgent-occupied area of Khao Kho during the years 1968 and beyond for several years.

The Mission of the Author

Even though the author viewed the assignment from the Thai Sangha to propagate Buddhism at that time as highly risky to personal safety, he saw it as an opportunity to serve the religion. In the name of Phra Maha Sompong Damdaeng Kunavaro, residing at Wat Mai Phiren, Pho Sam Ton, Thonburi, he traveled to carry out religious duties in the dangerous area of Khao Kho. The author spread Buddhism to various hill tribes living in the highlands. This mission received strong support from the government, and reaching out to ethnic minority hill tribes through religious activities proved to be unexpectedly effective. The author is considered highly successful as the head of the Thai Sangha's Dhammaduta mission under Mahachulalongkornrajavidyalaya University.

In addition to teaching Buddhism to various hill tribes, the author also served as a representative of the United Nations, educating the hill people on hygiene and public health. He taught them how to cut their hair, wash their faces, and brush their teeth. Most importantly, during that mission, the author gained the trust of the hill tribes, who entrusted him with bringing their children to be ordained as Buddhist monks at Wat Benchamabophit, numbering in the hundreds.

The author and Maha Samanera Maew were conducting a Buddhist ceremony to inaugurate a school in Khao Kho, Phetchabun Province, as an educational institution for the hill tribes, particularly the Hmong people, who had converted from animism to Buddhism. (Photo taken on May 4, 1968)

The author's efforts in assisting the hill tribes at that time received widespread recognition. The leading English-language newspaper in Thailand, *Bangkok Post*, conducted a special news feature on the author. This eventually led to a special interview with the U.S. Ambassador to Thailand, Richard Carpenter, when the author applied for a visa to pursue a master's and doctoral degree in the United States with a Fulbright Scholarship.

Admitted to violating the fifth precept of Pacitti.

At that time, bringing hundreds of hill tribe children to ordain in Bangkok was a task beyond the capability of the writer.

There was only one way to move hundreds of people from the jungle to Bangkok, which required protection from military forces and support from military vehicles.

The following story is about the quick thinking and resourcefulness of the author. It can be said that it was fortunate that the author decided to act, even though it was something that a Buddhist monk should not do, or if done, it would be considered a minor offense, even if it were trivial. However, from the worldly perspective, people might criticize this. The story goes that when the author, as the head of the missionary group, sought a meeting with the commander of the military forces at the camp, he introduced himself as a graduate of MahachulalongkornRajavidyalaya University in Bangkok. The military officer, a colonel who had spent most of his career in combat units in the jungle, did not have much knowledge of the outside world. He understood that the author, Phra Maha Sompong Dumdeang, was also an alumnus of Chulalongkorn University, just like him. With great pleasure, the officer offered the author a drink of alcohol as a gesture of friendship and spoke of unity and success.

This was a challenging decision, and at that moment, the choice could have gone either way. If the decision was correct, accepting the drink would have led to cooperation from the camp commander. Even though it violated the monastic code, it would have resulted in the commander's support. However, if the author had refused the drink to maintain monastic discipline, the military unit might not have helped with the transportation of the hill tribe members to Bangkok for ordination. This would have caused significant harm. For the greater good of the mission, the author chose to accept the drink from the commander of the military forces.

The writer's achievement as the leader of the missionary team in bringing a hundred hill tribe children to be ordained at Benjamabophit Temple in Dusit District is considered a major success. Major newspapers covered the event in their news reports.

The mass ordination of hill tribe people was the first of its kind, and the writer was the first person in the Thai monastic community who successfully led a large group of hill tribe people to be ordained in Buddhism.

Why is it called "Khao Kho," and where is it located?

It is called "Khao Kho" because the area is rich with a type of tree that has palm-like leaves but produces fruit resembling betel nuts. These trees are commonly found in the Khao Kho area, where the climate remains cool throughout the year. The Mhong hill tribe people often use the leaves to cover their house roofs.

Khao Kho Peak has an elevation of 1,174 meters, and on the same mountain range, there is another peak with a lower elevation of 990 meters. This peak, located to the west, is known as Khao Pang Kor. People in the surrounding areas commonly refer to the area as "Khao Kho Pang Kor."

Khao Kho is located in the upper part of Phetchabun Province, with the following adjacent boundaries:

To the north, Khao Kho borders Nakhon Thai District, Phitsanulok Province; to the west, it borders Dan Sai District, Loei Province, and Lom Sak District, Phetchabun Province. To the south, it borders Mueang District, Phetchabun Province.

To the west, Khao Kho borders Mapprang District and Wang Thong District, Phitsanulok Province.

Currently, Khao Kho is one of the 11 districts of Phetchabun Province, having been upgraded to a district on June 19, 1991.

Returned to visit Khao Kho again in the year 2016 (B.E. 2559).

The author visited Khao Kho for the first time as the leader of the first generation of Thai Buddhist missionaries in the year B.E. 2511 (1968). It was during a period of intense conflict with the Communist Party of Thailand insurgents.

After the author left the area, following the intense conflict with the communist insurgents, the author traveled to study in the United States and Canada. The author then settled in the United States for over 50 years. When the opportunity arose, the author planned a trip to return to visit Khao Kho again.

Why did the author have to travel back to visit Khao Kho again?

In November 2014, while sitting and talking by the campfire at the author's house in Portland, Oregon, USA, the participants in the conversation included the author, Patty (the author's wife), Pichin Thongmee (a former associate labor judge who immigrated to the US over 30 years ago and became a US citizen), Sarawat Jareuk Samasangsi (a former border patrol officer who served in the southern region until retirement, and now has passed away), and Tom Intharakiat Rodpradit (the author's assistant).

In the conversation that day, the author shared stories from the past when he helped various hill tribes as the head of the first group of Thai Buddhist missionaries sent by the Buddhist clergy through Mahachulalongkorn University to work on religious activities. The author mentioned that he must return to visit Khao Kho again for two purposes.

The first purpose was to reminisce about the past, and the second was to complete the thesis the author had previously submitted to the University of British Columbia in Canada. The author invited and made a promise to his dear friend, Intharakit Rodpradit, who had helped the author write several books, to join him on the trip as a companion.

In the end, the author decided to travel back to Thailand. Before departing, the author informed Tom, a dear friend who had been in contact through both email and other means, about the decision to return.

The author regularly communicated via LINE, informing that the arrival in Thailand would be on December 7, 2016, at Suvarnabhumi Airport. From there, the author would continue traveling by domestic flight to Chiang Mai, accompanied by a niece. The author intended to reward the niece for completing her bachelor's degree in military science from Oregon State University, USA.

Ultimately, the dream became a reality.

The daily life of the author and their assistant involved exchanging information, including articles. The author would write in English and send it to Tom, their friend, to arrange for publication in various books they co-wrote. Tom would translate and edit the material for accuracy before inserting it into the respective stories. The author also informed Tom that they would return to Thailand on December 7, 2016, landing at Suvarnabhumi International Airport before continuing on to Chiang Mai with their niece. This trip had two main objectives.

The first objective of the author was to reward their niece, who had graduated with a bachelor's degree in military science from Oregon State University. This was to make their niece's dream come true, as she had always dreamed of visiting Chiang Mai to ride an elephant, just as she had imagined.

The second objective of the author was to return to visit Khao Khor once again and take the opportunity to invite their dear friend, who had been assisting the author in writing various books, to visit Khao Khor as well.

Activities during the stay in Chiang Mai.

Kraai had a dream of visiting Thailand, the land of her grandfather Danny's birthplace, and she strongly desired to visit and ride an elephant at least once in her life. The writer himself had always had a love for animals, and this would be an opportunity to ride an elephant as well.

Kraai went to ride the elephant, which was her dream, and she was very happy.

Kraai climbed onto the back of the enormous elephant with pride, without any fear. However, what was funny was that the writer fell off the elephant. Instead of helping, the person who saw it just laughed and chuckled.

After the writer and Kraai spent time traveling in Chiang Mai, especially taking Kraai to fulfill her dream of riding an elephant, the writer wanted to go to Khao Khor immediately. However, the writer couldn't go because of a promise made to Tom, their dear friend, during his visit to the writer in America. The promise was that if the writer had the chance to return to Khao Khor, Tom would be taken along.

The first activity of the writer upon arriving in Chiang Mai was enjoying Thai food after a long period of being away, as shown in the picture.

The problem at that time was that the writer had to fly from Chiang Mai to pick up Tom at Suvarnabhumi Airport, then transfer to Don Mueang Airport to travel to Phitsanulok, and finally take a rented minivan to Khao Kho. However, things didn't go as planned due to a flight schedule issue. The flight from Chiang Mai to Suvarnabhumi was delayed by an hour, and upon arriving at Suvarnabhumi, we had to wait in a long taxi queue to get to Don Mueang. The feeling was that the booked flight from Don Mueang was about to take off soon, but the taxi queue was still long. The writer complained aloud that even though there was a plane ticket, they probably wouldn't make it in time for the flight.

Luckily, the writer still had some good fortune. When the taxi queue staff overheard the complaint, they asked what time the booked flight from Don Mueang was scheduled to depart. Upon learning that the departure time was very close, the staff decided to let the writer cut in line ahead of other passengers, allowing them to catch a taxi to Don Mueang in time.

It was a funny incident that occurred when the writer followed the staff. Kraya, the writer's granddaughter, who was carrying the luggage, tried to catch up with the staff. The staff quickly shouted, "No, No, Not you!" not believing that Kraya, who appeared to be of Western descent, was the writer's granddaughter and had traveled with him. This was because the grandfather and granddaughter had different skin tones and features (as shown in the picture).

When the writer explained and confirmed to the staff that Kraiya was indeed her real granddaughter, they finally accepted it. We got the taxi as requested. The taxi driver understood our need to make it on time to catch our flight from Don Mueang to Phitsanulok. Since it was a Friday, traffic was heavy even on the expressway. It was nothing short of a miracle that we managed to check in just 20 minutes late, and at that time, the plane had not yet taken off. The ground staff, however, did not allow us inside despite negotiations. She explained that it was the passenger's responsibility to arrive on time and that the advance payment for the tickets could not be refunded.

The writer was very upset that they did not receive good service from the airline. Not only did they miss the flight that day, but their group also had to pay extra for the overnight stay at the Amari Airport Hotel and additional costs for the flight to Phitsanulok with AirAsia. Despite these problems, it did not deter the writer from their desire to return to visit Khao Kho with their friend Tom and Kraiya, their granddaughter.

The writer and their assistant on Khao Kho had a view of the long mountain range stretching behind them.

When they arrived in Phitsanulok, they rented a van to Khao Kho for 1,700 baht per day, with the driver included. The writer felt a bit surprised by the rental arrangement, as in America, the renter would typically agree with the car rental company to cover fuel costs. However, in Thailand, the renter has to pay for fuel, which required some negotiation. They were somewhat fortunate to have a driver who was a man of ethics, introducing himself as someone who had worked as a driver for a Buddhist organization for many years.

The driver, Mr. Sannan Phuiket, not only drove them but also acted as their tour guide. He took them to visit various places, including Khao Kho Temple and other temples, as time allowed, just as the writer had planned from the beginning.

We stayed at the Imperial Resort and Hotel, which is a standard-level hotel. It provided excellent meals throughout our stay, as shown in the image.

The writer was spending their free time drinking and discussing work plans, which covered several topics. Although we only stayed at this hotel for a short period of three days, Mr. Sannan, the driver, was able to take us to visit several important places, including a visit to Wat Khao Phatthanarama to pay respects to Phra Kru Phatcharakana Phibul, the abbot and district chief of Lom Sak.

The writer was puzzled as to why Phra Kru Phatcharakana Phibul, the abbot of Wat Khao Phatthanarama in Khao Khor district, also held the position of district chief for Lom Sak, which is a different district. The driver, who had close ties to the national Buddhist office, explained that the administrative position of a district chief monk did not necessarily have to be restricted to the temple located in that district.

The writer visited and paid respects to Phra Kru Phatcharakana Phibul, the abbot of Wat Khao Phatthanarama and the district chief monk of Lom Sak.

The writer, Khraiya, and Tom took a photo in front of the portrait of Phra Kru Phatcharakana Phibul, the district chief monk of Lom Sak, as they visited during a time when Phra Kru was receiving invitations from other provinces.

The writer has a long-standing relationship with Phra Kru Phatcharakana Phibul, dating back to when the monk was newly ordained as a novice in Songkhla province. The writer had been instrumental in providing assistance to him. However, due to bad luck, the writer was unable to meet him on the day they had planned to pay respects. They learned from the temple's staff that Phra Kru was engaged in an invitation ceremony in another province and would usually return after several days.

The writer left some common medications that they had brought from the United States with the temple staff, asking them to offer the medicines to Phra Kru when he returned. The temple staff accepted the medications and assured them that they would deliver them once the monk was back at the temple. The writer had previously been close to Phra Kru, which made the gesture meaningful.

The writer was once very close to Phra Kru Phatcharakana Phibal during the time the writer was ordained as a novice. The writer also played an important role in assisting Phra Kru during that period. Here is a brief introduction to Phra Kru's background:

Phra Kru Phatcharakana Phibal (Klaew Thanissaro)

The writer and their assistant took a photo with the image of Phra Kru Phatcharakunabhidharma, the abbot of Wat Khao Patthana Ram, and the district chief monk of Lom Sak District, Phetchabun Province.

Currently, Wat Khao Phatthana Ram is a center for meditation practice for those visiting Khao. In the past, this area was a bloody battlefield. Today, there are still memorial sites for visitors to come and reflect on the history.

Luang Phor Klaew Thanissaro.

He holds the position of abbot of Khao Khao Phatthana Ram Temple, Khao Khao Subdistrict, Khao Khao District, Phetchabun Province, and the district abbot of Lom Sak.

The reason he is a good practitioner and respected is because, in the past, he was a thief. He lived a life of robbery and caused harm to others. However, he was a thief who had a change of heart, laid down his weapons, retired from his criminal life, and turned towards the monkhood.

In the southern border provinces, about 40-50 years ago, when people heard the name "Sia Klaew," everyone would quickly lock their doors in silence because they feared harm. The life story of Luang Phor Klaew, the abbot of Wat Khao Khao Phatthana Ram, is briefly told as follows: he was the twin brother of Luang Phor Klai, the abbot of Wat Nam Tok Thammaros, Rayong. However, fate seemed to play a role in shaping his life, starting in a rough way but ending well.

He was born in the village of Hua Thin, Tambon Phang Yang, Amphoe Ranod, Songkhla Province. He lived a life typical of someone with little means. At the age of 12, a group of bandits stole 40 of his family's buffaloes and even harmed his mother and older brother, whom he loved dearly. This caused great resentment, and he joined another group of bandits seeking revenge.

He then learned the ways of banditry, including spells and magic. He stayed with the bandits for about 8 years.

When he was about 20 years old, his relatives begged him to surrender to the authorities. Eventually, he agreed. Since no one dared to be a witness, all the charges against him were dropped.

Seua Klaew abandoned his wicked ways and turned to the good path by becoming a monk, following the advice of his elder brother, who was a monk. He devoted himself to studying and eventually completed the PhD 4. He learned meditation practices from the 5th Wat Mahathat and became proficient. Afterward, he made amends by helping people and supporting many relatives whom he had wronged in the past. Seeing his sincere efforts to do good, his relatives forgave him.

In 1979 (B.E. 2522), Phra Maha Klaew Thanissaro, who traveled from Songkhla Province, came to renovate Tham Sombat (formerly known as Tham Ruesi) in Bungsueng Subdistrict, Lom Sak District, Phetchabun Province, as a memorial for future generations. At that time, Phra Maha Klaew had been involved in the restoration of the site and created permanent structures.

Including one Dhamma hall, one bell tower, one dining hall, seven nun's quarters, ten bathrooms and toilets, the Phra Kan Shrine, the Deva Hall, a water storage tank, a Naga staircase, and a large principal Buddha image. The construction was completed in 1984 (B.E. 2527), after which he relocated.

Later, he undertook a wandering ascetic journey (tudong) and eventually took residence at Wat Khao Kho Phatthanaram to provide aid to the families of those he had once harmed in the past. Over the decades, he transformed into a meditation master, becoming a revered and trusted spiritual figure for the people of Phetchabun.

While residing at this temple, he developed and established a meditation practice center within the temple grounds. As a meditation master, he taught mindfulness and meditation, attracting disciples from both near and far who regularly traveled to study Dhamma with him.

On December 5, 2015, he was granted a royal promotion in monastic rank to Phra Khru Sanyabat, a special-level district monastic chief, under the title Phra Khru Phatcharakhanaphiban.

One long-standing practice is organizing alms-offering meals for monks on the last Sunday of each month.

Luang Por Klaew said, "I have seen the difficulties faced by monks in rural areas, far from urban development, particularly regarding the four requisites for their sustenance. The shortage of food and necessities forces monks and novices to travel long distances to the city in search of sufficient provisions for their monastic life."

Luang Por Klaew, therefore, invited monks and novices to receive the great Sangha Dana at Wat Khao Kho Phatthanaram.

The funds raised from the grand merit-making event are allocated by Luang Por Klaew to establish a scholarship fund for monks and novices at Mahachulalongkornrajavidyalaya University, Phetchabun Provincial Classroom, located at Wat Phrasond Sakkaram.

He is indeed a highly respectable monk.

A certain amulet journal once praised him as the "Deity of Khao Kho."

The writer feels immense pride for having played an important role in providing assistance and having been part of the journey that guided his life. At one point, he turned his life around from being a notorious bandit to entering the monkhood as a novice in Buddhism. He became a revered practitioner who earned the respect and reverence of Buddhists in Phetchabun province and surrounding northern provinces.

The background is that Phra Athikarn Kling was closely acquainted with Professor Maha Phrom. As a result, Professor Maha Phrom entrusted Phra Athikarn Kling with the responsibility of taking care of novice Klaai, who was sent to study with Professor Maha Phrom at Wat Hua Pom in Songkhla province. The writer recalls that Professor Maha Phrom and Phra Athikarn Kling asked him to look after and take on the role of a senior novice to care for novice Klaai, even though Klaai was older than the writer. Novice Klaai had previously been a notorious bandit who had killed and robbed people before becoming a novice to atone for his sins. Professor Maha Phrom mentioned to the writer, "Please take care of him; we are from neighboring villages, Pung Yang and Pung Tree, and are very close. And Professor Serm Thirapunyo is also your teacher."

Phra Athikarn Kling spoke of his familial ties, and the writer was asked by both teachers to assist as a tutor, particularly in guiding novice Klaai through teachings in the Dhamma and Buddhist scriptures, helping him study with diligence. They ensured that novice Klaai would learn grammar and foundational texts properly. The writer also took novice Klaai to study the higher levels of Pali at Wat Leab. Novice Klaai trusted the writer and accepted him as both an older brother and a special teacher in his life. One day, novice Klaai requested the writer to accompany him on a visit to his younger brother.

While Khlai was imprisoned in Songkhla Province, novice Klaai told him, "You must stop doing bad things, my younger brother. I have a disciple who is a novice Pong, who is always there to help me.

I am currently studying the Dhamma and training my mind with novice Pong. Novice Pong has come to ask for help.

Let go of all the bad things from the past and make a fresh start. After you get out of prison, come ordain as a monk, my younger brother. This is the intention that novice Pong had when he came to visit you."

Later, after Klaew was released from prison, he followed the intention set by novice Pong and was ordained as a monk. Both of them became leaders in raising funds to support and renovate the temple with the help of their teachers. They also built a sermon hall. The writer feels very proud of both students.

Both Maha Klaew and Maha Klang were recognized in the *Lokthip* magazine as prominent monks and spiritual leaders in Thailand. The writer feels proud and content to have been part of their lives, serving as the foundation for the good deeds they carried out. Both monks have greatly contributed to the Buddhist faith and the nation. On one occasion, the writer, along with P'Chin Thongmee and his wife Nong Da, visited Maha Klang at the Dharma Rots Waterfall Monastery in Rayong. Maha Klang had built a large monastery with various statues of Buddha in different poses.

In December 2016, the writer returned to visit Khao Khao as planned and traveled to see Maha Klaew at Khao Khao Phatthana Ram Temple, accompanied by the writer's assistant, Intharakiet Rodpradit, and Khaiya, the writer's niece. Unfortunately, the visit did not go as expected. Upon arriving at the temple without prior notice, the writer met with the monk's assistant, who informed them that Maha Klaew was away attending a religious event in another province. Typically, when Maha Klaew accepts invitations to events in other provinces, he is away for several days. Although the writer did not meet him, they left behind some essential medicine brought from the United States, as well as a book in English titled *21st Century Buddhism* as a gift for Maha Klaew. The writer hopes to return to the temple in the future to personally pay respects to him.

Phra Tamnak Khao Kho

Phra Tamnak Khao Kho is a royal residence located on Khao Ya in Sado Phong Subdistrict, Khao Kho District, Phetchabun Province.

Phra Tamnak Khao Kho is a royal residence where His Majesty King Bhumibol Adulyadej the Great, Her Majesty Queen Sirikit the Queen Mother, and members of the royal family stayed. It is located on Khao Ya, at an elevation of 1,100 meters above sea level. The residence was built by government officials, police, and military personnel after the war had ended.

With deep gratitude for His Majesty's benevolence, the local people in the northern region gathered funds to construct Phra Tamnak Khao Kho after the armed conflict with the communist insurgents had ceased. It was built as a symbol of encouragement for the local people and served as a working residence where the King and the royal family would stay when visiting royal projects in the Khao Kho area.

Inside Phra Tamnak Khao Kho, the structure consists of interconnected buildings arranged in a circular shape. There are quarters for royal officials that connect to the main residence. The buildings feature a curved design with two floors. On the upper floor, there are two large bedrooms serving as the royal sleeping quarters.

The upper floor contains two large bedrooms, designated for His Majesty King Bhumibol Adulyadej the Great and Her Majesty Queen Sirikit, the Queen Mother. The lower floor consists of a royal banquet hall, with a kitchen located at the front, as well as a dining room, an audience chamber, and a grand hall.

Additionally, the lower floor also serves as the bedchamber for Somdej Phra Srinagarindra, the Princess Mother, Her Royal Highness Princess Maha Chakri Sirindhorn, and Her Royal Highness Princess Chulabhorn Krom Phra Srisavangavadhana.

In front of the royal residence, there is a landscaped garden with circular flower beds. At the center of the circular layout stands the Maharaj Flagpole, which is 60 meters high. This flagpole was erected to commemorate the 60th birthday anniversary of His Majesty King Bhumibol Adulyadej the Great.

The construction coordinator was General Pichit Kullawanit, and the designer was Mom Luang Tritot Yut Thewakul. The engineer in charge was Dr. Rachot Kanjanavanit, while the construction was carried out by Lt. Col. Theerawat Swamiwasdhu (supervisor) of the 4th Engineer Battalion.

The project had a budget of 26 million baht without using government funds and took just over seven months to complete. The official opening took place on February 25, 1985.

Apart from visiting Khao Kho Palace and the Memorial for the Fallen Heroes, our group also had the opportunity to admire the stunning sea of mist.

Khao Kho today is completely different from the first time the writer visited. In the past, when the writer first set foot there, it was a battlefield between Communist insurgents and government forces, resulting in many casualties and injuries. It was considered a forbidden land due to its high risk. This stands in stark contrast to the Khao Kho of today.

Today, in 2016, Khao Kho has transformed into a paradise for tourists. It is a popular travel destination with well-developed attractions, drawing a large number of visitors each year. This visit to

Khao Kho also gave the writer the opportunity to complete their research paper that had been pending for submission to the University of British Columbia, Canada, fulfilling their intention.

The writer met with Nong Prapas and Nong Sommai on Khao Kho.

The writer considers it not a mere coincidence to have had the opportunity to meet both Nong Prapas and Nong Sommai on Khao Kho after being apart for more than 50 years. Rather, it was the result of the bond the writer shared with both of them during the time they lived in Wat Mai Phiren Phothisamton. At that time, Thanonburi was still a separate province and had not yet been incorporated into Bangkok as it is today. Both were students at Wat Mai Phiren Phothisamton under the guidance of Ajarn Ha Thongkham, and they studied at Thaveethapisek Secondary School together. Prapas and Sommai were under the care of their beloved teacher. The writer can say that they played a part in resolving misunderstandings between the two during that time. Later, Prapas mentioned, "If Brother Sompong had not intervened in the fight between him and Sommai that day, he would surely have been talking to Yama (the King of Hell) by now."

Prapas once suffered from an inflamed appendix and had to undergo urgent surgery. The surgery went smoothly. Afterward, most patients typically need rest and peace, but Sommai enjoyed reading books. Whenever Sommai read, he would make noise by tapping with a stick to create rhythm and atmosphere for his reading. However, Prapas, who was recovering from surgery, couldn't tolerate such noise and requested Sommai to stop making sounds, directly confronting him.

The more Sommai increased the frequency of the noise, the more it became a breaking point for Prapas. Prapas thought that Sommai was either doing it intentionally or playing tricks on him, which led to a challenge between them. He reflected that a young person who was recovering from surgery might react violently if no one intervened. He realized that if Phī Neng Sompong hadn't walked by and seen the situation, stopping the confrontation, Prapas himself would surely have ended up in the hospital.

Afterward, Prapas graduated with a bachelor's degree in history from Mahasarakham University, retired from his position as the director of a primary school in Ajsamarn District, Roi Et Province, and became the owner of a large organic farm in Roi Et Province.

As for Sommai, he is a civil engineer who graduated from Lat Krabang and pursued a master's degree in engineering at Chulalongkorn University. He retired from his position as a chief engineer at the Department of Highways and is currently a consultant for a major private construction company.

Both of them, along with their families, willingly traveled hundreds of kilometers to visit the writer at Khao Khor. The writer was deeply touched by their kindness, as it reflected the love and bond they shared.

After we finished our sightseeing tour and when the time was right, we set off back to Bangkok with an AirAsia flight. At Suvarnabhumi International Airport, Tom had to part ways with the writer and his companion. The writer and his companion boarded a connecting flight to Hat Yai to join the writer's family, who had already traveled ahead.

The welcome party for the writer was held at the home of the writer's sister in **Pak Kret, Nonthaburi**.

The farm of the writer's siblings is located in the **honey garden, Ratchaburi province**.

The house is located in Ch. Chang Chara, Kanchanaburi Province.

The project to address the issues faced by elephants was initiated with the support of a compassionate landowner who allowed their land to be used for the project. This location has become an eco-tourism site dedicated to elephant conservation, especially for elderly and wandering elephants. It provides an opportunity for people to get close to the elephants, learn about their lifestyles, and interact with them in a natural setting. Additionally, the center acts as an educational space for both tourists and volunteers.

The Kanchanaburi Elephant Conservation Center, or "Ch. Chao Elephant Sanctuary," is located in Village 4, Nonghoi, Wang Dong Subdistrict, Mueang Kanchanaburi District, Kanchanaburi Province. It was established in May 2008 by Dr. Samart Prasitphol, the head of the Animal Health Development Group at the Kanchanaburi Provincial Livestock Office, who has been closely involved with elephants throughout his career at the Department of Livestock Development.

He recognized the various challenges faced by elephants, including injuries, aging elephants experiencing health care issues, and wandering elephants. Many of these elephants are considered "unfortunate," unable to work at elephant camps. Thus, he sought a place to address these challenges, a place that would provide proper care for the elephants, have a natural environment, and sufficient water sources to support them.

The project to address the elephant issues was initiated with the support of a landowner with a compassionate heart, who allowed the use of their land for the project. This location serves as an eco-tourism site focused on caring for elderly elephants and providing a sanctuary for wandering elephants.

It offers a place where people can get close to the elephants, learn about their way of life, and engage with them in a natural environment. The site also provides an opportunity for tourists and volunteers to experience and contribute to the well-being of the elephants.

The elephant lovers aim to ensure that Thai elephants live a healthy life surrounded by the beautiful nature of Kanchanaburi. Activities at the sanctuary include planting food crops for the elephants, such as bananas, sugarcane, pineapples, pumpkins, and grasses. The elephants are also bathed and cared for, ensuring their well-being.

Currently, the Ch. Chao Elephant Sanctuary cares for a total of seven elephants, including six resident elderly elephants and one wandering elephant that was entrusted for care by Bangkok.

The Prisoner of War Cemetery, Kanchanaburi Province

35

Erawan Waterfall, KanchanabuProvince

Visit the Lipe Island Group, Satun Province

The author visited Lipe Island many decades ago. In the past, the island's natural environment was a forest with no development. However, today, it has become an important tourist destination that has been developed in all areas, much like Khao Kho.

Lipe Island, also known as Koh Lipe, is an island located in the sea within the area of Koh Sarai Subdistrict, Mueang Satun District, Satun Province.

It is situated to the south of Adang Island, approximately 85 kilometers from the mainland of Satun Province. The island falls under the jurisdiction of the Tarutao National Marine Park in Satun Province. The island features beautiful beaches with clear and clean seas, making it a peaceful and serene destination.

The author and their family spent time traveling to various islands in Satun Province, with most of their time spent on Lipe Island. Afterward, our group took a flight from Hat Yai to Suvarnabhumi Airport and then continued on to Portland International Airport to return home in the United States.

Visit Khao Kho

For more than 50 years, the author had the opportunity to visit Khao Kho again, as intended, after the author had left the red area that was called in those days as 'forbidden land.' It was the territory of terrorists who wanted to establish a communist regime in Thailand.

There were fights between insurgents and government officials by the year 1965, communists were in the form of an organization called "The Communist Party of Thailand" and used the abbreviation "CPT." They first infiltrated in to Khao Kho Hin Rong Kla by extending to the mass and ethnic groups who have been unfairly treated by the government.

The Day of Gunfire

In the beginning, The Party of Communist of Thailand lilied on some groups of Hmong Hill Tribes as the mainstay in expanding its base by means of propaganda and emphasizing then propagated that the authorities would take revenge and kill all the villagers, causing fear that they migrated to join with the Khao Kho terrorist group from then on, then attacked government's base several times, causing the majority of the mass to be afraid of and also with their propaganda, the mass has migrated into the forest to join the terrorist group and established RGW state authority, then there was a fight with government authorities, causing many of military, police forces and civilians dead and wounded. Then, the state cracked down on terrorists in many areas, covering the area of Chon Dan district, Petchbun.

Province, Maprang District, including parts of Nakornthai District of Phitsanulok Province.

Fighting between a group of terrorists and government authorities at that time caused great damage, killing civilians. The military and the Police forces created a panic situation that showed no sign of easily ending.

The author is the head of the first Dhammaduta Missionary group of the Thai Sangha.

The Thai Sangha realized that the threat of terrorists affected the safety of lives and properties of the people in the area, especially the livelihood of the hill tribes. Therefore, the Thai Sangha has a resolution to establish the Dhammaduta group to preach Buddha's teachings to the hill tribes are to eject hill tribes from terrorist groups. In addition, it will be the best way to bring Buddhist teachings to them and propagate them from terrorists. It will lighten the burden of the state as well.

The Sangha committee is concerned about the monks who will carry out the mission in the red area to get the best results must be senior monks who have at least 5 rainy seasons.

The author's name was submitted to the Council of Dhammaduta for consideration but was rejected at first consideration with the reasons that the author is a junior monk and does not meet the qualification of having 5 rainy season. However, the Council of Dhammaduta can not find any monk who is competent and qualified to lead the Dhammadut group under the guidelines led out by the Singha council. Finally, the author's name was resubmitted to Chao Khun Phra Promkunaporn, Director of the Mahachulalongkorn University acting as President of the selection committee of Dhammaduta's group for reconsideration and at the same time, he was my own teacher, and he trusted in my ability to carry on mission assignment, and my name was finally approved.

The author's mission.

Although the author viewed that being assigned by the Thai Sangha to propagate Buddhism at that time would pose a high risk of safety, but the author sees it as an opportunity to pay back the gratitude to Buddhism.

The author in the name of Phra Maha Sompong Kunawaro, who lived in Wat Mai Pirentara, Dhonburi, traveled to perform religious activities in the risky area around Khao Klo and spread Buddhist teaching to various hill tribes in the highlands. The mission was well supported by the State. In reaching out to hill tribes minorities through religious activities was considered the best possible effective, beyond expectation. The author has achieved great success as the first group of Dhammaduta missionaries of the Thai Sangha supported by Mahachulalongkorn Rajvidhayalaya, Buddhist University of Thailand.

In addition, the author's duty was to teach hill tribes. The author was acting as a representation of the United Nations in educating them on how to maintain cleanliness in public health, wash their faces, brush their teeth, and have a hair cut.

The most important success of the author's activities in teaching hill tribes at that time is that the author was entrusted by the hill tribes population to ordain as Novices in Buddhism at Wat Benjamabophit; numbers of hundred.

The author's work in helping hill tribes at that time was widely mentioned the the leading English-language "The Bangkok Post," have covered the author's activities until known to the United State Ambassador to Thailand, H.E. Richard Carpenter, who asked for an interview the author on the occasion of the author's visa application to further study at the level degree of Masters and PhD, under Fulbright scholarship.

Agreeing to break the precept Prohibition of Pacitti

In bringing hundreds of hill tribes' sons to be ordained in Bangkok at that time was a big deal beyond the author's ability to do, and the only way to bring them who had faith in Buddhism who wanted to learn Buddhism teaching in Bangkok was to have closed corporation and protection from military force with their military vehicle support.

The following happened is the matter of intellectual ability of the author and could be said that it was a good luck for the author who had decided to do so, although, monks in Buddhism should not do of if done, it will be considered an offense, even if it is a minor offense in the precepts but is is called Logavatcha or Worldly criticism that is when the author as the head of Dhammaduta missionaries, asked to meet a commander of Military Forces at the Camp "Son" and when meeting with him who is in combat unit at the rank of colonel, the author introduced himself as a graduate from Mahachulalongkorn Rajavidayala, University in Bangkok, the commander very happy to welcome the author since he thought the author came from the same University due to the fact that during his entire career, he was posted in combat Unit in the forest that he may have no knowledge of the outside world that Chulalongkorn University and Mahachullongkornrajavidayala is different Universities, with his joy that we, both are from the same aluni then he offered the author a glass of liquor to drink and said for the friendship and for the unity of success.

It is a very challenging problem to make a decision at that moment if the author's decision was right, even if that decision was against the precept of discipline, the results will be satisfactory to get cooperation from Unit Commander of Camp "Son," however, if refused to drink, because the author must maintain the discipline, great consequences will be the results that effected that may have no cooperation from the Commander of Military unit to transport hundreds of children of hill tribes to be ordained in Bangkok, the author accepted to drink with the Commander and was entrusted from military unit by providing transportation vehicle to transfer hundreds of hill tribes children to Bangkok to be ordained at Wat Benjambophit as planned.

The author's work in the capacity of the head of Dhammaduta missionaries in bringing hundreds of hill tribes children to ordain at Wat Benjamaborphit at that time was widely mentioned, and all local main Newspapers have reported the success of the author's mission as the first head of Dhammaduta's missionaries of Thai Sangha.

Why is it called 'Khao Kho'? and Where is 'Khao Kho' located?

The name of Khao Kho is known as an area that is fertile with a type of trees with palm-like leaves, but the fruit is similar to betel nuts, which are common in the Khao Kho arear with the cold weather all year round. The Hmong tribespeople like to use thatch for the roof of their houses.

Khao Kho Peak has a height of 1174 meters, and on the same mountain, there is another peak with a lower height of 990 meters. The villagers, therefore, called it "Khao Kho Pang-ko."

Khao Kho is located in the upper part of Phetchabun Province.

North adjacent to Nakornthai District, Phitsanulok Province, Dan Sai District, Loei Province, and Lomsuk District of Phetchabun Province.

The west is connected to Maprang District and Wang Thong District of Phitsanulok Province.

Come back to visit Khao Kho again.

The author visited Khao Kho for the first time as the head of the first Dhammaduta, the missionaries of Thai Sangha, in the year 1968 and stayed there for several years. It was the area of terrorists from the Communist Party of Thailand who set up Insurgent Forces to fight the Thai state, causing a lot of loss of lives and property.

Later, the author left the red area that was called in those days a forbidden land, the area where the Communists terrorists wanted to establish communism in Thailand. There were fights with government officials, which caused many casualties, then, the author went to study in the United States of America and Canada and settled in the USA over 50 years. Whenever the opportunity arises, the author has made his plan to come back to visit Khao Kho again.

Why does the author wants to come back to visit to Khao Kho again?

One day in November 2014, while sitting in front of the author's campfire at 1138 S.E.Renolds Street, Portland, Oregon, USA, and the parties who join the conversation on that day are: The author, Patty, the author's wife, Chin Thongmee, a former judge in Thai Labour court who emigrated to settle in the USA for more than 30 years until receiving American citizenship, Lt.Pol. Jaruek Samang Sri (Formerly a border Police Officer posted in the southern area until his retirement, and he is dead now) and Intarakiart Rodpradit

The story of the conversation on that day, the author told the story of the past when he came to help various hill tribes as the head of the first batch of missionaries of the Thai Sangha through the University, Mahachulalongkrorn Rajavidayalay, who sent the author to perform religious activities and the author has foreseen that the author must return to visit Khao Kho again with 2 objectives:

Firstly, as a remembrance of memories of the story in the past and secondly, to fulfill the requirement the author's thesis submitted to British Columbia of Canada, and the author has persuaded and promised to bring Intarakiart Rodpradit, in his capacity of the author's assistant as co-writer of various books as traveling companion.

Finally, the author decided to come back to Thailand, and before leaving, the author informed Tom, whom we had been communicating with all along through email and Line, informing him that the author would arrive at Suvarnabhumi Airport on December 7, 2016, then going to connect domestic flight to Chiang Mai with Kyra, my granddaughter, because the author intends to award her on the occasion of her graduation from University of State Oregon with Bachelor degree in Food Science.

Chapter 6

Visit and pilgrimage in India

The author has been writing the original manuscript detailing their biography, achievements, and mission for a long time in preparation for publication. However, the manuscript turned out to be a rather large pocketbook. Therefore, the author decided to divide it into multiple volumes, including nearly 60 articles about significant individuals in their lives. The author believed this content would be sufficient for submission to the publisher.

However, an assistant, who is also a co-author of several books, including *Crisis... Conflict in the Three Southern Border Provinces* suggested that the author should also write about their visits and contributions to underprivileged communities in India and Sri Lanka. If omitted, it would leave the biography, achievements, and mission incomplete. The author strongly agreed with this suggestion and thus began writing further.

Although the author currently has limited time due to professional responsibilities, they continue to serve as a senior medical volunteer at the *Loy Ram* hospital ship. This vessel was converted by the U.S. Navy into a field hospital since the outbreak of COVID-19 and remains in operation to this day.

Additionally, the author dedicates a significant portion of their time to caring for Marley, their last remaining dog—a Border mix—who has been seriously ill for several months due to old age. Marley is now 14 years old.

Despite these commitments, the author is determined to complete writing about their life and experiences in both countries as soon as possible, aiming to finalize the work by Christmas. The author also intends to avoid a purely historical narrative, as doing so would result in an extensive volume. Instead, they plan to provide a concise account to facilitate the reader's understanding.

India

India is the second most populous country in the world, following only the People's Republic of China. It is one of the oldest nations, rich in history and diverse culture. Additionally, Buddhism, a significant

Religion widely followed by Thai people originated in India. The author, having visited India at least three times, wishes to write about the country from their personal perspective and experiences.

India (อินเดีย) or Bharat (ภารตะ in Hindi), officially known as the Republic of India, is a country located in South Asia, occupying most of the Indian subcontinent. It has the second-largest population in the world and is the most populous democratic nation.

India has the largest population in the world, exceeding one billion people. It has approximately 188 spoken languages. Economically, India ranks fourth in global purchasing power. Its northern border is shared with China, Nepal, and Bhutan. To the northwest, it borders Pakistan. To the east, it shares a border with Myanmar, while the southwest meets the Indian Ocean. The southeastern border connects with Sri Lanka, and Bangladesh is surrounded by India to the north, east, and west. Additionally, India's maritime boundaries extend to Thailand, Myanmar, and Indonesia. With a total area of 3,287,590 square kilometers, India is the seventh-largest country in the world.

History

The history of India originated from the Indus River Valley, which was the cradle of the first civilization of India, flourishing around 2,600 to 1,900 BCE. Later, around 2,000 to 1,500 BCE, Indo-Aryan people from Central Asia migrated to India and encountered the Indus civilization. The two civilizations merged to form Vedic civilization. The most significant evidence of this civilization is the Vedas, which are religious texts in Sanskrit and the foundation of Hinduism, including its legal system, governance, and customs. This marks the Vedic period. The Rigveda is the oldest Veda, followed by the Yajurveda, Samaveda, Atharvaveda, and the great epics like the Ramayana and Mahabharata, which were written around the end of the Vedic period, during the time of the Buddha. The Aryans in India originally lived as nomadic herders but later began farming, trading, and forming large kingdoms, leading to the establishment of a clear caste system.

Later, Islamic civilization began to expand its influence in India starting from the 8th century AD. Muslim traders from the Middle East and the Arab Empire sent armies to invade the Sindh region (now part of Pakistan). The most prominent empire at that time was the Mughal Empire (16th–18th centuries), which saw a vast expansion of Islamic influence, including in governance, language, architecture, art, and the spread of Islam.

During the reign of Emperor Aurangzeb, who was a devout Muslim, laws were enacted that caused conflicts between Hindus and Muslims, leading to resistance against the Mughal Empire. After his power diminished, the Mughal Empire gradually weakened and began to fragment, providing an opportunity for the British to rise to power. The British started exerting influence in the subcontinent in the 17th century, initially through trade and later by colonizing territories and interfering in local politics.

India came under British rule in 1877, with Queen Victoria of England holding the title of Empress of India. After a long struggle against British rule, led by Mahatma Gandhi and Jawaharlal Nehru, India gained independence and became a member of the Commonwealth on August 15, 1947, with the British monarch still serving as the head of state. A Governor-General was appointed to administer the country on behalf of the monarch. On January 26, 1950, the Republic of India was established, with a President as the head of state and Jawaharlal Nehru serving as the first Prime Minister.

In the hot season, with the blazing sun, at the front area of the library of Mahachulalongkorn Rajavidyalaya University, a Buddhist university located inside Wat Mahathat Yuwarajarangsarit on Thaprachan Road, Bangkok, the atmosphere is filled with tranquility. Beneath the Ashoka tree, which lines the area around the temple, the bright yellow robes of the monks and novices who are students of the university can be seen. They are standing and listening to the teachings of the teacher, which is a daily ritual, before allowing the novices to enter the classroom. The teacher would talk to them about who they are, where they come from, and the significance of being a student at the Buddhist university. It is considered an important opportunity for each of them, as it provides the chance for education for a better future. As students of this Buddhist university, they are trained to be thinkers and dream big. When they graduate, they will go into the world and bring both worldly knowledge and Buddhist teachings to teach the world. On that particular day, however, there was an announcement over the microphone. It was announced that novice Sompong Damdaeng had been selected by the university to receive a scholarship to continue studies at a prestigious university in India. Sompong will leave us to study abroad in this summer, and everyone was encouraged to congratulate him and offer support, wishing him strength and success in his studies, which would bring success to all of us and to the university.

The event that took place, the writer vaguely remembers, occurred in the summer of 1963 or around that time.

The writer had to prepare everything for the trip to study in India. However, since the writer had never traveled abroad before, the preparations were quite challenging. Despite this, the trip didn't create much excitement. On the contrary, the writer felt regretful for having to leave behind the research work and Vipassana teaching that they were passionate about.

What excited the writer about the trip to India was knowing that two senior monks would be traveling with them. Both monks, whom the writer deeply respected, were Venerable Phra Maha Phrom and Venerable Phra Maha Suchin. Although both were elderly, they had a strong enthusiasm to pursue their master's and doctoral degrees in India. Their goal was to gain knowledge that could help spread Buddhism in the future. The two monks' readiness to travel was far greater than the writer's. They had prepared everything necessary for the journey and even brought blank tapes to record their lessons for future listening. This was a clear sign of their readiness and advancement. In contrast, the writer hadn't prepared anything special.

When the writer arrived at the campus of Banaras Hindu University, they were warmly welcomed by the university staff. The staff responsible for international students provided guidance and helped with the registration process. While registering, the staff member said to the writer, "We are happy and proud that you have decided to study here. We all warmly welcome you.

As scholars in the field of Sanskrit, we consider Sanskrit to be our primary language, but it is an ancient language that modern generations don't pay much attention to. Young people tend to prefer studying technology fields because, after graduation, it's much easier to find a job and earn a good income. On the contrary, studying ancient languages, such as Sanskrit, makes it much more difficult to find a job. Therefore, modern generations prefer to study technology. However, since you come from Thailand and still have an interest in this ancient language, we are pleased to welcome you, and we hope that after you graduate, you will help our university teach Sanskrit to students and anyone interested in it. the writer responded with gratitude and also thanked the representative of the university. After completing the registration process, the writer returned to the dormitory.

Banaras Hindu University

Located in Banaras, Uttar Pradesh, India, this university is considered by the people of India to be the largest university in the country and the third largest in the world, with an area of 10 square kilometers.

The university spans 10 square kilometers, or approximately 3,750 rai. The perimeter of the university is about 15 kilometers, and it is administratively controlled by the central government. Additionally, it is recognized as a center for education, arts, culture, and various academic disciplines in

India. Scholars from all over India and abroad travel to study and conduct research at this prestigious university, including the writer.

The origin of Banaras Hindu University (B.H.U.) began with the visionary idea of a great man named "Pandit Madan Mohan Malviya." He was born in 1861 in the city of Allahabad, which is 125 kilometers away from Banaras.

At that time in India, the air was filled with the spirit of nationalism, led by the Indian National Congress. Malviya dedicated himself to this great cause and worked to instill a sense of Indian identity in the hearts of the younger generation. By engaging directly with the people, he realized that true independence wasn't just about gaining freedom from foreign rulers but about preserving the rich traditions and culture that had been passed down for generations. To achieve this, he understood the need to cultivate a sense of awareness in the younger generation in order to build a new society. This would require a comprehensive university.

The ideal university, according to Malviya, should have two main characteristics: first, it should integrate the technological advancements of the West with the intellectual wisdom of the East. This means it should not blindly follow Western models or cling too strongly to traditional ideas of its own. Instead, it should be able to select the best elements from both worlds and apply them for practical benefit.

In 1890, Malviya held a meeting to gather ideas for...

In 1890, Malviya convened a meeting to gather ideas from prominent scholars and notable figures in Allahabad, with strong support from the Maharaja of Varanasi, Prabhu Narain Singh, and the then Lieutenant Governor of Uttar Pradesh, Sir Anthony McDonald. As a result, the Hindu University Board of Governors was established.

When the university was actually established, Varanasi was chosen as its location, covering a vast area of over 3,000 rai. The reason for selecting Varanasi was that it is a cultural hub of Hinduism, with Hindus making up about 97% of the population in India. The university's purpose was also to preserve and promote Indian culture directly.

Currently, the university offers courses through three institutes, 14 faculties, and 114 departments. One of the popular fields of study is Ancient Languages, with Sanskrit being a highly sought-after discipline for those interested in studying India's traditional culture, including the writer. There are more than 30,000 students from over 40 countries enrolled across all institutes and faculties.

When the writer enrolled in the master's program and chose Sanskrit as the primary subject in the first term, they received top grades in all subjects. The professors were highly pleased with the writer's academic performance and offered the writer an opportunity to assist in teaching Sanskrit. The writer accepted the offer without hesitation and began helping to teach Sanskrit to students interested in this ancient language. Additionally, the writer assisted professors teaching Sanskrit to enhance their teaching skills in the language. It is noteworthy that the writer...

The Sanskrit teachers, both from Europe and Asia, included many from Germany and several from Japan as well. These students were often monks, novices, and nuns, with some hailing from different regions of India.

The students, including nuns and young learners, felt a close connection with the writer as a Sanskrit teacher. Some of the nuns even wished for the writer to become a monk, which would allow them to go on a spiritual journey to the Himalayas together. We set up camp on the hillside of the Himalayas to meditate and discuss philosophy and how to survive in the world. The philosophical discussions included the principle of Ahimsa (Nonviolence), a key philosophy championed by great figures like Mahatma Gandhi, who led millions of Indians to demand independence from England. Ultimately, India achieved independence. This principle of nonviolence also inspired Martin Luther King Jr., who sparked social change in America.

The principle of Ahimsa, or the philosophy of Nonviolence, as described by Dr. King in his first book, *"Stride Toward Freedom,"* states that he was inspired by Jesus Christ and the techniques of the great Indian leader Mahatma Gandhi. He outlined six key principles as follows

1. Principle One: Nonviolence is a way of life for courageous people.

1) It is active, nonviolent resistance to evil.

2) It is aggressive spiritually.

The first principle of Ahimsa states that nonviolence is a way of life for courageous people, which includes two key aspects.

The first principle is nonviolence, with the power to fight against evil.

The second principle is that nonviolence is a matter of the spirit, focused on determination and perseverance.

2. Principle Two: Nonviolence seeks to win friendship and understanding.

1) The result of nonviolence is redemption and reconciliation.

2) The purpose of nonviolence is the creation of the beloved community.

The second principle of nonviolence seeks to find a way for friendship and understanding, which means:

The first point: The result of nonviolence is aimed at compensation and reconciliation.

The second point: The purpose of nonviolence is to build a community filled with love.

3. Principle Three: Nonviolence seeks to defeat injustice no people.

1) Nonviolence recognizes that evildoers are also victims and are not evil people

2) The nonviolent resister seeks to defeat evil, not people.

The third point of nonviolence is: Seek ways to overcome injustice, not to defeat people.

The first point of nonviolence: Nonviolence accepts that those who commit evil are also victims, as they are not inherently evil people.

The second point of nonviolence: Nonviolence seeks to overcome evil, but not to overcome people.

4. Principle Four: Nonviolence holds that suffering for a cause can educate and transform people and societies.

1) Nonviolence accepts suffering without retaliation

2) Unearned suffering for a cause is redemption and. transforming possibilities.

The fourth principle of nonviolence: Nonviolence holds that suffering for a cause can provide wisdom and insight for both individuals and society.

The first principle of nonviolence: Nonviolence accepts suffering without retaliation.

The second principle of nonviolence: The suffering endured is seen as a withdrawal and a possibility for transformation.

5. Principle Five: Nonviolence chooses love instead of hate.

1) Nonviolence resists violence of the spirit as well as the body.

2) Nonviolent love is spontaneous, unmotivated, unselfish, and creative.

The fifth principle of nonviolence: Nonviolence chooses love over hatred.

Principle 1: Nonviolence opposes violence in all forms, both to the spirit and to the body.

Principle 2: Love that is nonviolent arises naturally and without motivation, free from self-interest, and is a constructive matter.

6. Principle Six: Nonviolence believes that the universe is on the side of justice.

1) The nonviolent resister has deep faith that justice will eventually win.

2) Nonviolence believes that God is a god of justice

Principle 6: Nonviolence believes that the universe is inherently aligned with justice.

Principle 1: Nonviolence holds a deep belief that, in the end, justice will prevail.

Principle 2: Nonviolence believes that God is the ultimate source of justice.

While the writer enjoyed teaching meditation and philosophy on the slopes of the Himalayas, deeply immersed in the experience of life with nature, having experienced true freedom as a wanderer, one day, the writer heard a broadcast from Thailand announcing that the writer had been missing in the forest for a long time. Anyone who found the writer was asked to inform the Thai radio station. The writer was always aware that their journey to India to study and teach at a university there was made possible by support from influential figures in Thailand. The writer felt a responsibility toward the mission they were entrusted with, so they decided to leave the group and return to Thailand after completing their studies with a degree in Ancient Language and Anthropological Archaeology.

The writer takes pride in having studied several ancient languages, including Pali, Sanskrit, and ancient Khmer. They had the opportunity to teach the knowledge of ancient Khmer at the doctoral level to students interested in ancient Asian languages at the University of Washington in the United States and the University of British Columbia in Canada.

After the completion of the memorial ceremony for Mother Indira Dumdeang, who passed away due to old age, on Saturday, July 4, 2004, at Khuan Ka Hong, Khuan Ka Hong District, Satun Province, Thailand, the author took his eldest daughter, Donna Dumdeang, and his wife, Patty, to visit and make merit in India. The author, as the president and founder of the Dumdeang Foundation, participated in building a hospital and an elderly care home, guided by Father Yesu, a renowned priest in India. The author, together with Betty Michael, President and Founder of GSM, sponsored Father Dr. Yesu.

At the GSM headquarters in Beaverton, Oregon, USA, during that time, the director of the GSM office from around the world attended the seminar. Father Yesu, whom the author selected as a sponsor for that occasion, was provided with a plane ticket to travel between India and the USA, along with accommodation, meals, and other necessary expenses. Father Yesu recently passed away in southern India. Before this, the author had traveled back and forth between America and India many times to monitor the progress of the construction of the hospital and the elderly care home. During the construction, the author wanted his wife and daughter to see firsthand what the hospital and elderly care home buildings looked like, how many buildings and rooms there were, and how they assisted patients, both children and adults of all genders and ages, as well as how the elderly care home helped the elderly in southern India.

This pilgrimage trip was undertaken by the author, his wife, and their three children, making it a pilgrimage journey (Pilgrimage) as practiced by many Muslims for a long time. We boarded a plane from Don Mueang Airport in Bangkok to Chennai (old airport).

The flight took about 4 hours with Thai Airways, and we had purchased tickets from an Indian airline. However, we ended up flying with Thai Airways instead, possibly due to an agreement or contract between the airlines, but we are not sure the writer had booked first-class tickets for Patty, his wife, and Donna, his eldest daughter. However, the writer chose to sit in business class. There is something the writer would like to document about the trip. In business class, there was a group of young Muslim men, and one of them was seated next to the writer. As soon as the writer sat down, they greeted him, saying, 'Sir, where are you traveling to?' The writer replied, 'I am going to Kolkata but will stop at Chennai first.' They smiled and said, 'We are all getting off there too. We can tell by your appearance that you are a happy person, and we would like to offer you a drink if you don't mind.' The writer responded, 'Thank you, I appreciate the kindness from all of you.'

At that moment, the writer became suspicious of the behavior of the young Muslim men and thought to himself that if they had any hidden intentions or were planning anything harmful, his knowledge of Thai boxing, which he had learned from his boxing teacher, Nimmit, from the southern region, might help protect the lives of Patty and Donna, as well as the captain and other passengers on board. So, after calming his mind, the writer accepted the drink from the group of young Muslims, who numbered around 10. Among them, one man introduced himself as being from Phatthalung province. His group consisted of doctors from Thailand traveling for a medical seminar on tropical diseases in Chennai. Since they had never traveled abroad before, the writer gave them advice on how to fill out forms, go through immigration checks, and what to do upon arrival. This made them very grateful, and they ordered drinks and food for the writer as a gesture of appreciation.

They said they had never seen an older person who appeared as friendly and content with life as the writer. The writer informed them that he was always happy to offer help and provided them with his phone number and email. They all thanked the writer profusely, and the writer has continued to stay in touch with some of the young Muslim men from that group, even to this day.

When our flight landed at Chennai Airport, Father Dr. Yesu was there to welcome us. He felt very happy to receive us and took us from the airport to the train station in Cathy, from Chennai to Kolkata. This brought back memories for the writer, reminiscent of traveling from the Hat Yai train station, where everyone was trying to make money from us, asking if we had any luggage, and so father Dr. Yesu told us that everything was in a manageable state. We were in a sleeper train, and there was nothing to worry about. Donna liked the sweet tea from India that came in cans, and she would drink it often, enjoying it until she needed to use the bathroom. She felt extremely anxious about the train's bathroom, almost fainting from fear. She was so startled that her clothes got drenched, and the dollar bills in her wallet also got soaked with waste. We didn't know the full story behind what happened to her until we checked in at the hotel. The train took us to the city where Father Dr. Yesu lives, traveling throughout the whole day and night.

We booked a stay at the largest hotel in the city. The hotel had the largest swimming pool, almost as big as the Olympic pool, which made Donna very happy. The bellboy refused to leave the room until we gave him a tip. Coincidentally, I didn't have any cash on hand. I looked at Patty, and she didn't have any either. I looked at Donna, and she didn't have any because her dollar bills were soaked. However, paying a tip was still necessary because it's a tradition. So, I told Patty and Donna.

We paid only what we had, which solved the problem. Both Patty and Donna started laughing together. The fact that Donna's dollar bills were soaked with water from the bathroom became a funny story that we still talk about to this day.

Donna felt very happy to stay in the large hotel. She exclaimed to the writer that it was a big hotel with a lot of colors. The writer had a large office, while Donna and Patty had big beds as well. The children mostly lived a beautiful life, as Donna smiled happily. The writer and the group were invited to go sightseeing and enjoy a fancy dinner. Donna had to call her friends in America almost every hour because she couldn't sleep well. Donna made a memorable note about her visit to India, which I find interesting, so I will share her writing below without translation.

After no sleep, we flew to Chennai, India from Bangkok. We got into Chennai – I met Dr. Yesu. Then we went to the Salvation Army, where there was no toilet paper + no soap. I took a short nap, and we went to eat Indian food at a nice hotel. Mom + I loved it! Papa, however, must be on a diet. He would talk about how good the food was (especially the "delicious" chicken) but look across the table at me, and make faces + say "Yucky!" Today begins the first day of my dad's weight loss plan.

After dinner we took 2 tuk-tuks to the train station. The driver told us we had to pay 1000 rupees because there was a white woman (Mom) in the tuk-tuk. Dr. Yesu got angry, then we proceeded to the train. We are currently on a train bound for Kakinda ("Co-canada") for THIRTEEN HOURS, with only enough toilet paper for 2 trips to the bathroom. 2 days from now, we'll be on the train again, heading to Hyderabad, another TWELVE hours!!!

It's all worth it though, because Papa got his book. It's beautiful – made us all get tears in our eyes. It's dedicated to Ya.

August 24, 2004 1:00 am

The train ride, which ended up being 14 hours long, was quite scary. We had sleeping ~~bunks~~ bunks, so it was fine while I was sleeping. The bathroom, though, was the worst part. The first time I went I thought the train was breaking apart. There I was in mid squat in an already not-so-comfortable bathroom, & the train tracks were crashing underneath me as the bathroom shook horribly. I was so scared, but I had to pee so badly! So I stood up, meanwhile relieving myself all over my feet & shorts! My underware & shorts were soaked, and I was still in this terrifying bathroom, shaking & rocking back & forth!! So I ran to our bunks, dripping the whole way, grabbed some clean shorts & changed right there in the hall of the train. Just dropped my shorts I didn't care — anything was better than that awful, scary bathroom. My mom said I probably would have gotten arrested standing there on the train in Holy India with no pants on!

After that incident, I would just lie there on my bunk (which was up high above my parents' ~~other~~ with two chains, to prevent falling) and

hanging from the ceiling

54

wait for the train to come to a stop
if I had to go to the bathroom!
Papa told us a funny story about
going to the bathroom himself! His
stories are always hilarious, especially
when he acts them out. Apparently we
were being too loud as Dr. Yesu
decided to sleep somewhere away from us!
He was gone in the morning!

We arrived to Kanikada, India at about
8:00 am (we left Chennai around 6:00 pm
the previous day). We were greeted by
Papa's friends - one of them a Pranan.
They gave us these beautiful, decorative
India necklaces. Put them around our
necks + welcomed us to Kanikada. One
of the men hugged Papa + said "Daney!
Oh Daney!". You can tell Papa's
so happy to be here in India. It's
nice to see him happy like this. He
is just glowing, + greets most anyone
he comes across.

We were taken to our hotel - Halcyon
Country Club. Very nice hotel - beautiful
marble floors + high ceilings. During
breakfast, Papa gave me his meal -
A grilled tortilla - like bread stuffed
with grilled onions. Mom loved it. I
thought it was good as an appetizer
(not as a main dish - not substantial
enough for me). Papa got out of

eating the Indian food & feasted on toast
& jam, while again talking about how
good the food was! So funny!

After breakfast I passed out for
5-6 hours. I didn't mean to sleep
my first full day in India, but
I was so tired from the past two
nights' lack of sleep.

After I woke up we went to find
a bank and check our email. The street
outside of the Halcyon ~~area~~ is busy
with tons of bicycles, tuk tuks, cars,
people, and cows!! White cows just
walking the streets! I'd always ~~heard~~
heard of this, but ~~to~~ actually see
it is another story! People respect
the cows & yield to them. The cows
just ~~walk~~ move slowly between
traffic — doing their thing. Drinking.
Shitting. Just being cows.

At 7:00 pm Dr. Yesu picked us up
to take us to his place for dinner.
We were greeted by 45 orphanges —
40 boys & 45 girls (or perhaps the
other way around) I think they
cried, "Praise the Lord" & gave us
these beautiful necklaces hand-made
of jasmine lillies, leaves, & tinsle.
45 huge smiles on these little children.
They lined up — boys on one side &
girls on the other. 45 kids. who.

were found homeless, without parents. Seeing them made me understand right at that moment why my dad spends so much time + money helping this cause in India. Again, he was just glowing. Smiling + talking to the children. It was amazing to see this. Just amazing.

We then went inside + had a very good dinner made by Aruna + Pinny, Dr. Yesu's wife + daughter. Papa finally ate! It was delicious. Thinking about ~~it now~~ it makes me hungry — so I'm off to bed with a growling tummy...

(~~Thank~~ Dona luck. Dona papa baby
dauther- you are the woman of the ~~guard~~.
~~Papa~~
Loves your ~~talk~~ and papa ~~feels closer~~

August 25, 2004   1:00 am

Papa ate today! We had delicious tandoori
& "tikki" chicken, and an onion salad
similar to thai som tum. Very good. Once
again, I am going to bed hungry, thinking
about food.

After lunch, Mom & Papa & I
went for a swim. The pool here is
large & deep -- there are strange
styrofoam -type balls floating all around.
Mom & I dove in the water while
Papa floated on an inner tube floating
device, telling us he was "letting
go" of Indian curry! We probably
wouldn't have been able to tell the
difference between curry & the styrofoam
balls! Anyway, Mom would dive off
the diving platform, while I was too
scared to dive in from that height
(about 2 feet, MAX above the pool -
what a wimp!). I will make it my
goal to dive from there tomorrow, if
we get a chance to swim.

~~After~~ swimming we checked our email
and got simosas & fresh-squeezed
juice before being picked up by
Dr. Yesu, who arrived an hour
later than planned - 8:00 pm. He
took us to the village where the
Calvary Prayer house is. The houses
there were ~~g~~ made of either stone

or straw! Straw huts. I'm sure there's something more than straw, but these were the most simple, primitive houses I'd ever seen! People and cows hung out outside the houses/huts. Many slept outside, as it's so hot here.

When we got to the prayer house, the people inside (mostly women + children) were singing + dancings. Many children came out to greet us. They love shaking our hands! They're so adorable — so young. They love to smile.

Inside the prayer house, Dr. Yesu introduced us all ("Donny" "Patty" "Doni") + talked about Papa's book + Papa's goals for the clinic + orphanages. The kids + women sang more songs for us — first girls, then boys, then women. Although I was dripping wet from sweat + was thirsty, — I enjoyed the singing — it was beautiful, even though I couldn't understand what they were saying

After the singing, we three got up to say a little something — beginning with Donny, then Patty, then Doni. Papa wore black to honor ya. He told the people about losing ya, + how he's sad, but still happy to

be here. Mom talked about always
wanting to come to India. I talked
about the beautiful, LARGE, leis
we were given (we got new ones tonight)
When the ceremony was coming to
an end, Papa & Mom & I passed out
bags of rice, grain, soap & dahl to
mostly elderly woman - women with
leprosy - women who could barely walk -
women who get one sari to where all
year. These are very, very poor people.
As Papa would say - "the
poorest of the poor."
After handing out the food & soap,
Dr. Yesu said a final prayer, then
directed us to walk out & shake
the people's hands. This shaking turned
into blessing. People came up to
me and asked me to bless them
by puting my hand on their
forehead. Women with small children
would ask me to bless their children.
A pregnant woman had me bless
her unborn child in her stomach. Kids
gathered all around. I felt so
akward blessing these women because
for one, I didn't know what I
was doing - and two, some would
pray for so long that I didn't
want to spend so much time

NO.

"blessing" them that I'd offend other people by either taking too long or by not "blessing" them the same way. I kept wanting to look for Mom + Papa, but didn't want to interrupt the blessing! As special as that was, I was happy to go back to shaking hands with the kids! At least I knew how to do that. Some kids kept on shaking our hands. Very sweet. Yep, they love to shake!

Papa's asked me a few times if I feel I'm in India yet.

Yes Papa — I feel as though I'm here. Seeing these people makes me see life so differently. It's such a different world. Even the moon hangs differently here!!

✗✗✗ Letter to Papa

August 25
10:30 PM
NO.

Dear Papa —

before I write an entry in this journal, I want to write a letter to you. And since I can't find any paper, I may as well write in this.

I feel so bad about earlier tonight, Papa. I am so sorry for disrespecting you & being rude to you. I know you always want what is best for me. I wish I knew how to step back & realize that before becoming argumentative with you.

Papa, I know this is the hardest time in your life I need to be a good daughter and not make things even harder on you. I apologize for arguing with you at all during this past month. I'm sorry for making you worry about me that night in Koh Samui (when I was out with Peter & Tommy). I realize that I am a selfish, disrespectful person & daughter. I want to change this about myself. Every time I do something I am not proud of — like today — I tell myself to think before speaking the next time I am faced with conflict/disagreement especially when it comes to you. I wish I wasn't the way I am. I feel so so bad, Papa. Please forgive me for being such a snotty daughter, especially now, when you need me the most.

NO.

I love you, Papa. I love you so much. I know there isn't a thing in the world you wouldn't do for me. You always keep your word to me, and I always seem to let you down. This is not who I want to be.

I promise when I get back I will begin re-paying the loan right away. This is one of many things I want to make right with you.

Losing Ya has shown us all how short & fragile life is. Just thinking of losing you or Mom makes me so sad I can't even stand it. Thus I want to make every day we have together as good as it can be — especially times like this, when I get to do something amazing with just you and Mom. Like the time I came to Thailand with you two — just the three of us. That was my favorite trip to Thailand so far.

Let's make the rest of this trip just as good, ok Papa? I don't want to waste any time being upset. I know I am stubborn as stubborn as they come! Sometimes I feel as though something inside of me comes out & acts this way, and I am watching it happen, not wanting it to happen but not stopping it.

Because I never want to hurt you or make you feel bad, although I know I often do.

I am so happy to be here with you and Mom. It _is_ a once-in-a-lifetime chance - one we may not have again. _I_ wanted to see your work here - the people ~~you're~~ you have helped - the children. I wanted to spend quality time with just you and Mom, like we did in Thailand. I wanted to see a new country. I wanted a new stamp in my passport! ☺

Today I was stubborn and impatient (2 of my ~~worst~~ worst qualities). Even when you offered a compromise -- when you said you'd buy me some pants- I was still unwilling to step outside of myself. All I could think at that moment was that you didn't care about my comfort. But I know you want me to be safe and not looked at the way I've been looked at here in India. You want the best for me, as always. I was upset when you said I would ruin the trip. I'm sorry, Papa. I will not ruin the trip. I promise. I want this trip to be a happy, wonderful, amazing trip with . . .

good memories & not of regret. Because I regret today. I regret treating you badly and disrespecting you. And I want you to know how sorry I am, Papa. I love you.

Thank you for coming and eating with us. Thank you for being calm and taking the step to terminate our conflict. I would be so sad if we were to continue being upset any longer than that. Even though I found myself upset and justifying my actions (like the stubborn, selfish person I am), I kept looking out the windows of the dining room at everyone who walked by, hoping it would be you. Please forgive me, Papa. Sometimes I just need to grow up.

I will wear longer clothes when I go outside of this hotel. I agree with you that I should. I'm sorry it took me so long to agree. I'M SORRY FOR BEING DISRESPECTFUL TODAY.

We have 4 days left in India. I want to make them enjoyable and memorable! I want you to know that I am fine with doing whatever you want to do here, whether it's going to New Dehli or Hyderabad, or Chennai, or staying here. I am happy to do anything. If you want to go to New Delhi, let's go! I just don't want you to spend so much for such a short time. BuT, like you said earlier today — its just money, and we'd get to see something new. It's up to you, Papa. I will do whatever, even if it means going on the train again!! (I'll know what to expect this time.) If going to New Dehli is what you want to do, then we should go. Mom + I came here to honor and be with you.

Once again I'm sorry for being a snotty, stubborn, selfish, impatient, disrespectful, rude person today. I will do my absolute best not to act in that manner again.

I love you so very much, Papa. hank you for this wonderful trip. d for taking us to Thailand. And r paying for Koh Samui, where I ad an amazing time — only we anted you to be there longer. ank you for the many flights e paid for during this lievable trip to d TWO different ries. I appreciate all you given me — I just need to it more.

NO.

I'm so happy I was here when you saw your beautiful book for the first time. I had to fight back tears of happiness when you got your book. I'm so happy I can be a part of your excitement, and ~~that~~ I'm honored that I'm personally in your book. I'm glad I can help bring your books back & be a part of promoting/selling them.
    I'm PROUD OF YOU, PAPA!!
    VERY, VERY PROUD.

I love you with all of my heart. Thank you for being there for me and for your never-ending support. Thank you for writing such kind things about me on the previous pages.

    I love you so much —
        Love always,
            Dora

    PS — Thank you very much for encouraging me & inspiring me to keep a journal!

August 26   12:15am

NO.

Today was relaxing and uneventful for me. I woke up & for the 2nd time this trip (1st time at Nidnoi's in Bangkok). I saw Papa's bare-naked butt. He was walking to the bathroom.

I got up at 12:30pm, as I had trouble sleeping the night before because I was so hungry! Mom & Papa were out doing banking again, getting money for the books. I ordered room service, then went to check my email. Ran into Papa there. I heard his voice over the stalls — he didn't know I was there.

Around 4pm, Papa & Mom went to Dr. Yesu's and watched some kind of teacher's ceremony and saw Dr. Yesu's mom. I decided not to go, and instead went to use the internet down the street (the one just down the street was not working). On the way to the internet place I realized that about half of the people were looking at me & the way I was dressed (spaghetti strapped tank top & shorts). They would literally look me up and down or take double and triple stares making sure they were seeing correctly! It was annoying and funny & uncomfortable and flattering all at once. What different cultures! I pictured myself as

Julia Roberts in "Pretty Woman" — the way people would look at her and stare because of the way she was dressed. A guy at the internet shop wasn't offended, though. I think in broken English/Indian he said I dressed "cute." He also said Indians don't like America. Thus, the next person who asked where I was from — I said, "Canada." Better. Nobody hates Canada!

On the way back to the hotel, I heard Papa call me from across the street at our juice stand. I joined them, and we all headed for the internet place so Papa could check his email. That's when he noticed the way people were looking at me. He told me I should wear longer clothes in India, and I became stubborn and defiant. We ended up getting into an argument.

I feel very bad about the way I acted to Papa. Ashamed, really. I wrote him a letter and I cried because I added to Papa's hurt & stress during this sad period of having lost Ya. I wish I could take my actions back. Luckilly though, Papa came back to the hotel (after I stormed off

like a little child) and joined Mom
and me in the dining room where we
were eating dinner. I'm glad he
did that. I didn't know what to
expect - would he be upset with me
and continue our conflict? Or we
he ignore me and pass right by?
He did neither. He came in and
sat down with us. He gave me
this journal and had me read the
kind + sweet things he'd written
about me and our time at Calvary
Prayer House the night before. We
talked, and that was that. We're
fine because Papa stepped up and
made the move to not allow our
conflict to go any further, this
makes me proud of him and
ashamed of myself for my actions.
To think - I thought he'd walk
right past Mom and me and
not join us. Proud of you, Papa!! Thank
you.

  After dinner we all went upstairs,
stuffed (although Papa mostly drank).
I think he had 2 pieces of the
chicken tikki, one of my favorite
dishes I've tried.

The next morning, we were taken on a tour to visit the orphaned children we had been supporting. They were staying in the shelter of Dr. Yesu. We also visited the central hospital of the large church. This continued for a week without any breaks, making us quite exhausted.

When we visited the orphanage, where hundreds of children lived within Dr. Yesu's shelter, Donna met an orphan girl whom she immediately liked and wished to adopt. However, due to our limited time, the adoption process could not be completed within the available timeframe.

In that church, our group presented gifts to every member of the congregation. We requested Dr. Yesu's team to prepare gift bags containing rice, soap, toothpaste, toothbrushes, handkerchiefs, and a certain amount of dollar bills.

Everyone eagerly responded, saying, **"Not yet, sir, I haven't received mine."** Even Dr. Yesu turned to me and said, **"Dr. Danny, please feel free to distribute the gifts as you wish."**

On that day, I met an elderly woman, over a hundred years old, who walked up to receive her gift directly from my hands.

Everyone applauded the elderly woman because, for many years, she had never stood up or walked since birth.

But that day… that moment… was the first time in her life that she was able to stand and walk.

It was truly a miraculous event—one that even medical science could not explain. Miracles can always happen through the grace and mercy of God.

After that, we departed from the church to request a meeting with the governor of an Indian state. The position is referred to as Legacy Officer, who is responsible for the entire region. If compared to a position in the United States, it would be equivalent to a state governor.

It was of great significance that Father Dr. Yesu, along with his team—who were both Brahmins and Hindus—led us to meet the governor, as shown in the photograph.

The governor was pleased and delighted to meet the writer. At the event, many local guests stood in line, waiting for an opportunity to meet the governor.

The governor was highly popular among the people. He first told the writer that he liked his church. The writer responded, "It was just recently completed, sir." The governor remarked that it was grand, colorful, and magnificent and considered it a great achievement of the writer.

Then, the governor asked the writer, "Dr., you were born in Thailand. Why do you hold American citizenship and come to help us Indians?

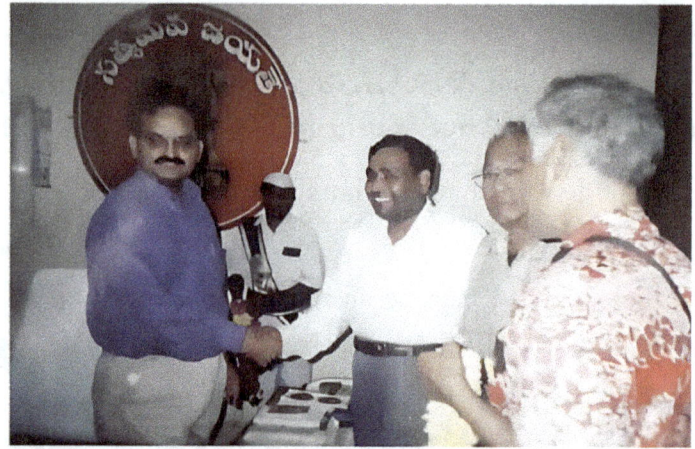

To establish a public health center for the elderly and build a hospital to provide healthcare services for underprivileged Indian communities. The writer responded to the governor, explaining that he had personally donated funds to construct a healthcare center for the elderly and a hospital to support underprivileged Indian communities. He had contributed a significant amount of money and requested that the people of the governor's region also donate in proportion to his contribution. The writer emphasized that his donations for these public welfare projects were not initiated by him alone but rather were a divine inspiration from God, who wanted him to assist the elderly and the less fortunate in Indian communities.

That means **God commanded the writer to help underprivileged Indians, using the writer as His representative.**

Additionally, **Mother Teresa** appeared in the writer's dream, speaking to the writer: "My child, I ask you to take on the burden of what remains, beyond what I have already done for the people of India. Please continue the work of helping the underprivileged." When the writer paid respects to the governor, he thanked the writer, hugged them, and said that the state would continue its efforts, expressing gratitude for the writer's personal donation to help create a service center for the elderly and underprivileged in the Indian community.

Our group expressed gratitude to the governor and bid farewell. After that, we traveled back to the hotel, and the following day, we returned to America.

The author takes pride in having the opportunity to help people in need, not only in the United States, India, and Sri Lanka but also in Thailand and other parts of the world, depending on the situation and necessity.

Chapter 7

Visit to Sri Lanka

Sri Lanka

Sri Lanka is a country that was once called Ceylon. It is made up of Sinhalese and Tamil people, and its official name is the Democratic Socialist Republic of Sri Lanka.

Sri Lanka is an island nation in the northern part of the Indian Ocean, off the southeastern coast of the Indian subcontinent. In the past, it was known as Lanka, Ceylon, and the Island of Ceylon during colonial times, a name that was used until 1974. It shares maritime borders with India to the southwest.

Sri Lanka is a country with a long history spanning thousands of years. It is a place where Buddhism, which originated in India, spread more than a thousand years ago. The country has experienced prosperity for a long time. However, it is unfortunate that there has been conflict and violence between the Sinhalese and Tamil people. When the writer became a Buddhist monk, they had a dream to come to Sri Lanka to further their studies of Buddhism. The writer felt immense happiness and inner peace when given the opportunity to meditate under a Bodhi tree in Sri Lanka, a tree originally from India and a central place of gathering for Buddhists in Sri Lanka for over a thousand years.

Although the writer once dreamed of studying Buddhist teachings further while still a monk, they did not have the opportunity at that time. This was because the writer received a scholarship from the Fulbright Foundation to pursue higher education at Washington University, one of the top 10 universities in the United States, at the master's and doctoral levels.

The writer had the opportunity to visit Sri Lanka for the first time after the great tragedy caused by the natural disaster of the tsunami (Tsunami) in Asia, including Thailand and Sri Lanka, on December 26, 2004. This tragedy brought great suffering to the people of Asia, with many individuals being affected and experiencing pain. A large number of people in history perished, and properties were destroyed. The writer reported on the devastating events that occurred during that time.

This is a copy of the report summarizing the efforts to assist victims of natural and flood disasters in Phang Nga, southern Thailand, which the writer organized. The writer has visited Sri Lanka several times and experienced several exciting events during their stay in Sri Lanka.

75

The first time, the writer was invited by the Supreme Patriarch of Sri Lanka to give a sermon to the Buddhist followers of Sri Lanka and also led a meditation session after the sermon.

The second time, the writer nearly lost their life when a helicopter entered the combat zone between the Tamil Eelam rebels and the Sri Lankan government due to intense conflict. The writer was a representative of the Red Cross, bringing aid to the minority group. It turned out that the helicopter the writer was in was shot at, but fortunately, they narrowly escaped unharmed.

Due to the writer's interest in the relationship between Siamese Buddhism and Sri Lankan Buddhism, which has developed over a long period of time, the writer presents the foundation of this relationship as the basis for further understanding as follows:

Buddhism in Sri Lanka, also known as the Lanka lineage (Buddhism from Lanka), has had a long and close relationship with Buddhism in Thailand. It is recognized as Siamese Buddhism or Buddhism, which originated in Siam.

The rise and decline of the Lanka lineage of Buddhism.

After the Buddha's parinirvana, three months later, 500 monks gathered to compile the teachings of the Buddha and conduct the first Buddhist council at the Sattapanni cave near the city of Rajagaha in the Magadha region. This council took seven months and marked the beginning of the Pali Canon, which forms the foundation of the Theravada Buddhist tradition. Around the year 236 BCE, Theravada Buddhism from India spread to Sri Lanka during the reign of King Devanampiya Tissa through the missionary work of the monk Mahinda, the son of King Ashoka the Great. Mahinda brought Buddhism to the city of Anuradhapura on the island of Ceylon (Sri Lanka). A large monastery complex was built at the Maha Megavana garden, where monks resided. King Devanampiya Tissa also sent a delegation to the royal court of King Ashoka to request that Queen Sanghamitta, a nun, come to Sri Lanka to ordain women and establish the first order of Buddhist nuns (bhikkhunis). Additionally, the sacred Bodhi Tree from the Buddha's place of enlightenment was brought to Anuradhapura. This period is considered a golden age for the development of Buddhism in Sri Lanka. In 238 BCE, King Devanampiya Tissa acted as a patron for the fourth council, which lasted 10 months and became the foundation for the Mahavihara sect. Later, during the reign of King Tuththakaminī and King Wātthakamini, the Pali Canon was compiled and transcribed onto palm leaves for the first time. There was also a division in the sect, leading to the emergence of the Abhayakīrīvāsī school (Sajphoomi Lao, 2556).

In the year 433 CE, King Rakkhita Mahathera convened the fifth council of the Tripitaka, which lasted one year, resulting in the first written compilation of the Tripitaka. Additionally, in 956 CE, King Mahānāma held the sixth council, and in 1584 CE, King Parākramabāhu conducted the seventh council. Several countries, such as Burma, Siam, and Cambodia, traveled to copy the Tripitaka for study. This period also saw the unification of the Mahāvihāra and Abhayakirivāsi sects, which had previously been separated. Furthermore, King Parākramabāhu established the first Sangharaja to oversee the clergy throughout the country. This period is also considered a time of great Buddhist temple construction and architecture, which became central to Buddhism.

However, after the Tamil invasion from India and the subsequent colonial rule of the Portuguese and Dutch during the colonial period (1953–2005), the Christian missionaries in Colombo forced Buddhist monks to convert to Christianity, and Buddhists were compelled to embrace Christianity. Buddhist temples and the Tripitaka were destroyed, leading to the gradual decline of Theravada Buddhism in Sri Lanka (Sombunboon, 2560; Sajphoomi Lao,2556)). Additionally, the Portuguese established a center for trade in Colombo, forcing King Dharmapala and the queen to convert to Christianity (1585–1624). Catholic missionaries took permanent control of temples. During the reign of King Rajasinghe I, monks and novices were executed, and the people feared giving alms to monks and novices. Buddhists had to conceal their religious practices until the Dutch took control of Sri Lanka in 2200 CE, beginning a restoration of Buddhism, and they sought assistance from monks in Siam (Sajphoomi Lao, 2556).

The study by Predee Hongstun (2560) provides information that during the 19th century after the British took control of Sri Lanka, they attempted to seize the land of the Buddhist clergy who had held it for a long time. The British also interfered in the internal affairs of the Kandyan monks by signing the Kandyan Convention in 2358 BE, which caused dissatisfaction among the Buddhists. This led to protests against the British, resulting in the suppression of the people in 2362 BE. Later, in 2391 BE, the monks led another protest against the English missionaries, as they refused to accept the spread of Christianity and the establishment of Christian missionary schools in Sri Lanka. This was accompanied by a strong sense of nationalism among the Sinhalese, who regarded Buddhism as a long-standing national identity. This gave rise to a struggle against the British. A key figure in this resistance was Anagarika Dharmapala, who was a leader in the revival of Sri Lankan Buddhism and founded the Maha Bodhi Society in 2434 BE. The goal was to establish a Buddhist university and publish Buddhist literature in various languages. Three important monks who played significant roles in this movement were Maha Thera Hikkatuwe Sri Sumangala, Maha Thera Migettuwatte Gunananda, and Maha Thera Veheragama Sumangala, who protested against the spread of Christianity.

In addition, Colonel Henry Steel Olcott (1832-1907), an American who founded the Buddhist Theosophical Society, played a significant role in the revival of Buddhism in Sri Lanka. After he converted to Buddhism, he was able to lead many Buddhists in Sri Lanka to join the Buddhist revival movement. He became an important force in opposing Christianity in Sri Lanka. He supported the idea of making Vesak Day a public holiday and helped design the universal Buddhist flag. He also raised funds to establish Buddhist schools to compete with the missionary schools. In 2424 BE, he published a book.

The *Buddhist Catechism* was created to be used as a teaching tool in schools and to give Buddhism a scientific approach (Bond, 1988). Berkwitz (2003) explains that Buddhism in Sri Lanka today has adapted to economic and political conditions, which have influenced the way of life of the people, particularly the efforts to return to its original roots as in the past. There has been a growing interest in pilgrimages to sacred Buddhist sites, as well as the integration of beliefs from other religions into Buddhist rituals to address the needs of living in a society where people must interact with others of different nationalities and religions.

The arrival of the Lankavamsa in the Siamese land.

Michael Wright (2001) mentions that it is presumed that Lankavamsa Buddhism first arrived in Siam during the reign of King Li Thai (around the 20th Buddhist century), passing through the Khmer region. However, through the examination of documents, inscriptions, and various archaeological evidence, it is observed that the entry of Lankavamsa can be traced in three phases:

1. The Dvaravati period (around the 10th to 15th Buddhist century), where traces of religious sites such as the Srimahosot city in Prachinburi, with architectural features similar to those in Sri Lanka, were found, as well as the Emerald Pond Temple, where footprints resembling the popular footprints in Lanka were discovered. In addition, the inscription at the pond of the Emerald Temple in Pali language mentions the year 683 (1304 CE) with the words "Lankissaro," referring to the King of Lanka.

2. The Khmer period (around the 15th to 20th Buddhist century), where evidence of a main Buddha statue was found in the Prang, the main sanctuary of King Chaiwaraman's Prasat of the seventh kingdom (1724-1753 CE). The Buddha statue is in the ancient Lankan style, similar to the stupas from the Polonnaruwa period, as well as the Buddhist relic stupa in Nakhon Si Thammarat (in the Tamphron Link city). It is believed that during this period, the Khmer had contact with Sri Lanka through Nakhon Si Thammarat as a connecting route.

3. The Sukhothai period. (During the 19th-20th Buddhist centuries) The construction of Lankavamsa-style stupas was observed, and King Li Thai adopted the Lankavamsa sect from the Khmer people. The stupas were designed in the shape of a Khmer-style prang (tower) and also included a unique design resembling a rice offering bowl, which was a modification of the Sri Lankan stupa style into the Khmer prang form.

The study states that Siam adopted the Lankavamsa Buddhist tradition in the 18th Buddhist century (during the Third Council of the Tripitaka) and flourished in the city of Nakhon Si Thammarat. According to the legends of Nakhon Si Thammarat and the Phra Boromthat Nakhon Si Thammarat, groups of people from Sri Lanka migrated and settled in the area of Phra Wiang within Nakhon Si Thammarat, bringing the Lankavamsa Buddhism with them. This tradition was practiced (Chatchai Sukrakarn, 2548). Additionally, Siamese monks traveled to Sri Lanka for ordination, and Sri Lankan monks returned to establish a monastic community in Nakhon Si Thammarat, where they also constructed the Phra Maha That Chedi. King Chanthraphanu of Nakhon Si Thammarat visited Sri Lanka twice and brought the Phra Buddha Sihing from Sri Lanka to enshrine in Nakhon Si Thammarat (Sombun Bunrith, 2560, pp. 42-43).

Subsequently, King Ramkhamhaeng sent monks from Nakhon Si Thammarat to spread Buddhism in Sukhothai and established their residence at Wat Aranya. The Lankavamsa Buddhist tradition spread to other areas. This continued until the reign of King Phra Chao Uthumphon of Ayutthaya (2275-2231 BE), a period when Buddhism in Sri Lanka began to decline. King Sri Vijaya Rajasinhha sent envoys to Siam and invited monks to restore Buddhism in Sri Lanka. The key figures in this effort were Phra Upali Thera, Phra Ariyamuni, and Phra Mahanaama from Siam, who brought Siamese Buddhism to Sri Lanka during the reign of King Kittisiri Rajasinhha (Phra Brahma Bandit, 2556; Phra Sri Thawat Methi,

2556). They sent a delegation of 61 monks to Siam, who arrived in Ayutthaya in May. 2294 . The monks from Siam then traveled to Sri Lanka in2296, with King Kittisiri Rajasinhha's blessing.

King Kittisiri Rajasinhha welcomed the Siamese monks and provided them with residence at the royal park, which was later established as Wat Buppharam. There, a ceremony was held to ordain six novices, marking the first ordination of Siamese monks in Sri Lanka. The first monk to be ordained was a novice named Kob Bakattu, the abbot of Wat Poy Maluvihara (Sombun Boonrit, 2560, p. 48-49). During the three years spent in Sri Lanka, Phra Upali Thera and his group ordained over 700 monks and more than 3,000 novices from Sri Lanka. Later, in. 2298, King Phra Chao Uthumphon of Ayutthaya sent a second delegation of 60 monks to Sri Lanka to propagate Siamese Buddhism. They taught the chanting of mantras, monastic practices, sermons, and meditation and introduced the Perahera (the procession of the sacred relic), which involved a procession with music, performances, torches, and elephants carrying sacred relics for Buddhist worship. The Perahera has become a beautiful and important tradition for the people of Sri Lanka until today (Sombun Boonrit, 2560, p. 49-50).

Since the Seventh Council in Sri Lanka in 1584 during the reign of King Parakramabahu, which was the last council of Sri Lanka, Siam has continued the tradition of convening the Buddhist Councils. The eighth council was held in 2020 during the reign of King Tilokaraj, with Phra Dhamma Titi Maha Thera as the chairman. It took place at Wat Photharam in Chiang Mai. The ninth council was held in 2331at Wat Phra Sri Sanphet (Wat Phra Mahathat Yuwarat Rangsarit) under the patronage of King Phutthayotfa Chulalok, with the Supreme Patriarch (Sri) as the chairman. The tenth council took place in 2431 at Wat Phra Sri Rattana Sadsadaram, with King Chulalongkorn the Great as the patron.

In. 2530, Somdet Phra Mahasaman Chao, Prince Phawaret Woriyalangkorn, presided over the 11th Buddhist Council, which was held at Wat Phra Mahathat Yuwarat Rangsarit. His Majesty King Bhumibol Adulyadej served as the patron, and Somdet Phra Sangharaja Sakon Mahasangkaparinayok (Vasnavasano) was the chairman (Sombun Boonrith,2560, p.40).

In2556, the Thai and Sri Lankan governments organized a celebration marking the 260th anniversary of Siamese Buddhism in Sri Lanka. The event used the Saturday of the full moon day in the eighth month of the year 1796 (B.E.2296) as the foundation date for Siamese Buddhism in Sri Lanka. On this day, Somaneh Kobbagattuve, the abbot of Wat Poyamaluvihara, was ordained as the first Siamese monk in Sri Lanka. Phra Upali Thera from Siam traveled to Sri Lanka to be the ordaining preceptor (Sajphoomi Lao,2556).

Chapter 8

Visit to Jamaica

Jamaica

Jamaica is a country located on an island in the Caribbean Sea. It is 240 kilometers long and 85 kilometers wide. It lies 625 kilometers to the east of Central America and the mainland, 150 kilometers south of Cuba, and 180 kilometers west of the island of Hispaniola, which is home to Haiti and the Dominican Republic. The Cayman Islands are located approximately 215 kilometers to the northwest. Jamaica is the third-largest island in the Caribbean, following Cuba and  Hispaniola. The population is around 2.7 million people. The country was once under Spanish rule and later became a British colony. The majority of the population is of African descent.

Most Thais recognize this country by the name "Jamaica."

The author is a travel enthusiast who has traveled to almost every country around the world. Every time the author goes on a trip, they feel excited and keep the memories, especially from island countries, including Jamaica in the Caribbean. The author has long had the intention to visit this country, and the author's sponsor resides in Jamaica. This sponsor is Professor Dr. Russell Grukkle.

The author and Dr. Grukkle have worked together at Washington University. Dr. Grukkle is a professor of ophthalmology, the head of the ophthalmology institute, and the chairman of the committee selecting graduate students for master's and doctoral programs at Washington University. The author is a lecturer teaching law and Southeast Asian studies.

During the time the author and their family had to return to Thailand for a period of three and a half years, communication was lost. During that time, Dr. Grukkle moved to settle in Jamaica. Later, the author traveled from Thailand to take up a teaching position at Washington University and has since settled in the United States.

Dr. Grukkle supported the author's research on the topic of the conflict between white (British) and black (local Jamaican) people stemming from social inequality in Jamaica. He invited the author to visit him, and the author purchased tickets through Horixon Agency, accompanied by the author's family: Patty, the author's wife. Donna, the eldest daughter, and Anna Cook, the author's adopted daughter, who served as a secretary. Dr. Grukkle arranged for the author's team to stay at his luxurious resort, providing an ideal setting for the author to conduct the research. Dr. Grukkle kindly provided a writing desk for the author to work on the history-related project.

Famous for his book *The Root*, Alexander, the author of this well-known book, lent the author a copy during that time to be used as a research desk. It was a great honor for the author to have completed the research report within the specified time frame. The outcome of this research has contributed new perspectives, creating new ideas in the context of globalization.

The author holds Dr. Grukkle in high esteem. Not only is he an expert in his field of ophthalmology, widely respected in both academic and general circles, but he is also genuinely passionate about the arts. Additionally, he has a deep interest in Buddhism, which he has spread in Jamaica by supporting the establishment of a Thai temple there. He is a philanthropist, having supported the underprivileged, including disabled individuals, in mainland China during his time as a teacher there, and he continues to support those in need.

In Jamaica, Dr. Grukkle has gained widespread recognition and high respect from the Jamaican people. His reputation is not only acknowledged in the general society but also in government circles, where he is highly regarded and trusted.

The author proved Dr. Grukkle's high regard in the government circles by personal experience. Once, the author traveled alone from Portland, flying to Texas without any luggage. Upon arrival, immigration officers initially denied entry because the author had no travel bags or luggage. However, after asking why the author had no bags, the author explained that the luggage had already been sent ahead to the destination. When asked where it had been sent, the author mentioned that it was sent to Dr. Russell Grukkle's resort. This was enough to allow the author immediate entry into the country.

Special lecture at Kingston University, Jamaica.

The author was invited to give a special lecture by the Chancellor of Kingston University, a leading university in Jamaica, on the topic "Social Inequality and the Principles of Buddhism."

The Chancellor, the university executives, faculty members, students, and the respected people of Jamaica.

In the opportunity when the writer visited Jamaica, the writer was invited by the Chancellor of Kingston University, which is the leading university in Jamaica, to give a special lecture on the topic, "My impressions on participating in the exchange of knowledge and understanding of the plant species and perspectives on Buddhism and social issues in Jamaica."

I feel greatly honored to be here today, standing before such distinguished individuals, thanks to the kind invitation from the Chancellor of Kingston University, which is the leading university in Jamaica. I would like to express my sincere gratitude for the warm introduction and the opportunity to speak at this esteemed gathering. I would now like to take a moment to introduce myself briefly.

I am originally from Thailand, born in a country located in the Asian continent. I have been interested in Buddhism since a young age and studied Buddhist texts at a university in Thailand before continuing my education at the University of Washington in the United States, where I earned a Ph.D. in Law. I was appointed as a faculty member at the university, teaching law for several years. Additionally, I received a scholarship to pursue further studies at the University of British Columbia in Canada in the Post Graduate Studies program. As a result, my English accent may be slightly difficult to understand compared to yours, as I have inherited my linguistic heritage from the English-speaking community.

Before coming up to the stage today, I had the opportunity to converse with the Chancellor, the faculty members, students, and the general public. I was deeply impressed by the warm reception, which made me feel as though we had known each other for a long time. The atmosphere was very welcoming, friendly, and close-knit, particularly in the context of intellectuals and education. The atmosphere in your country, especially, is similar to that of Thailand, and the kindness shown by all of you reminds me of the warmth of the Thai people. Professor Cook has also conducted research on countries in Asia, including Thailand, and has introduced fruits and plants from Thailand, such as the Sia tree.

Which you refer to as Bread of Fruit or Bread tree, etc. We, therefore share similarities in history between Thailand and your country, Jamaica.

I understand that at the University of Kingston, there are courses in religious studies, and several professors have expertise in Buddhism, possibly even more so than I do. I don't fully understand why I was invited to give a lecture on religion. The answer lies in the exchange of knowledge and ideas, which may differ. I am aware that the majority of Jamaica's population adheres to Christianity as the main national religion, followed by Hinduism, Buddhism, Islam, and a belief in ancestral spirituality. I feel proud that the people of Jamaica hold religion in such high regard, as it brings peace and harmony.

Before delivering this lecture, I had the opportunity to visit a Burmese temple in Kingston, Jamaica. I met with the abbot, who honored me by inviting me to give a lecture on Buddhism in conjunction with Vesak Day. I gladly accepted the invitation with great enthusiasm.

Vesak Day commemorates significant events in the life of the Buddha: his birth, enlightenment, and passing into Nirvana. The core teaching associated with these events is the Law of Nature, or the Three Marks of Existence: Anicca (impermanence), Dukkha (suffering), and Anatta (non-self). These three principles explain that everything in the world is subject to change suffering, and cannot be controlled by any individual will. Even the Buddha, the supreme teacher of the world, was not exempt from these laws, showing that no one can escape the fundamental nature of existence.

The three principles that can be exemplified on Vesak Day are gratitude, impermanence, and mindfulness.

All humans born on this earth share similar feelings. That is, we all despise injustice, love righteousness, hate suffering, love happiness, hate conflicts, and love peace. This is what we call human morality. Dharma is the universal ethics of all nations, languages, races, genders, and ages, not limited to any one religion. Only those who practice Dharma will achieve peace and happiness. Practicing Dharma leads to unity (Harmony), and only those who practice it will understand each other. Dharma, therefore, leads individuals to peace and happiness.

On this occasion, I would like to extend my best wishes to all of you who are participating in this gathering, and may peace and happiness be with you all.

Chapter 9

Visiting Cancun Beach and Tulum Beach

Mexico

Mexico is located in North America, south of the United States, with its capital being Mexico City. It serves as the country's political, economic, cultural, and transportation hub.

The charm of this. capital city lies in its impressive buildings and the fusion of ancient charm with the bustling atmosphere created by its large population, which is the highest in North America

Mexico is a country rich in food, culture, and historical monuments that reflect its thriving civilizations over thousands of years. Additionally, it is home to some of the most breathtaking beaches in the world. With more than 500 beaches stretching across the Pacific Ocean, the Gulf of Mexico, California Bay, and the Caribbean Sea, it offers a wide variety of coastal destinations.

Mexico's coastline features various types of beaches, with some serene spots surrounded by forests and ancient ruins that are thousands of years old. Along the coast, there are beautiful sandy beaches that, in the writer's opinion, are the most stunning in the world. The waters are calm, making them perfect for walking, meditating, or even thrilling wave surfing, which can rival the best spots globally.

Question: Why must it be Cancun Beach and Tulum Beach? Why not choose other places?

Answer: Because it is suitable for relaxation, yoga, walking along the beach, and tourists who want to have fun and enjoy activities like kayaking or increasing their adrenaline levels by playing kite surfing.

There are many types of entertainment venues in this vast land. Compared to Koh Chang or Koh Lipe, it is much larger. Both the geography and the areas are different.

The entire beachfront area is occupied by hotels or eco-bungalows, similar to the mountain resorts in northern Thailand. The level of service varies, and if you are looking for affordable prices, you can travel to the beach.

You can travel by taxi, or younger travelers often prefer to rent bicycles. Tourists can also travel from Cancun Airport by bus, depending on your convenience.

Cancun and Tulum beaches are considered two of the most beautiful beaches among the 15 beautiful beaches along Mexico's coastline, which has a total of 500 beaches. Traveling from Portland, Oregon, USA, where the author resides, is easy. The author, who loves traveling to various countries around the world, praises both beaches in Mexico for their stunning beauty and unforgettable experiences. The author has vivid memories of visiting these two beaches, especially the wedding ceremony of their eldest daughter, Donna, held in Tulum in 2017. The event brought together family, relatives, and friends from both the United States and Thailand, making it an unforgettable and memorable wedding.

At the wedding celebration of Donna Damdaeng, the eldest daughter of the author, and Jane Powell, held on the beach in Tulum in 2560, the event attracted widespread attention from the Mayan community. As a scholar in Buddhist studies, the author was asked to organize a Buddhist prayer ceremony alongside the Christian wedding rituals. The Buddhist ceremony was beautiful and impressive, leaving a lasting impact on both the local Mayan people and international tourists. According to a local Mayan newspaper, the wedding was reported as the most magnificent one ever held on the island, possibly the first and last large-scale wedding of its kind on this island or in Mexico.

The author has brought the Buddhist wedding culture in cooperating with Christian wedding culture as the Buddhist scholars. The author was asked to have a Buddhist mantra chanting along before the Christian wedding ceremony. Mayan News has reported that it is one of the best wedding ceremony performances on the Island among the Mayan Community. Buddhist chanting was fantastic and highly impressive to native Maya and foreigners that never ever have had in the history of Tulum Island and will never be again. It will be the first and the last of the best of the best wedding ceremonies in the island or entire nation of Mexico.

Cancun Beach

Cancun is the most famous beach in Mexico, with a length of 14 miles. It is located 131 kilometers away from Mexico City, which is a 2-hour and 28-minute drive. The beach has some of the finest white sand in the world and crystal-clear water. However, historically, this beach was once the site of ancient Mayan civilization and has many ancient tourist attractions. In this area, you can find a variety of corals when you go snorkeling or diving in the shallow and deep waters. Tourists enjoy activities like kayaking, fishing, and paddleboarding.

The author enjoys kayaking because, during the time they were pursuing their PhD at the University of Washington, they often took Patty (who at that time was just a fellow student in the author's class and not yet married to them) kayaking on weekends at Seattle Bay.

This beach has many restaurants, both indoors and outdoors, where you can try a variety of dishes. Cancun can be compared to the Las Vegas area in the United States due to its resort and hotel standards, which are quite similar. When you travel to Cancun, you will feel the same love for it as the author does.

Tulum Beach

During the visit to Cancun and Tulum, the author, along with Patty and their family from both the United States and Thailand, stayed in the Riviera Maya, a tourist and resort area located south of Cancun, Mexico. Riviera Maya is well-known for its large, all-inclusive resorts.

The author has interviewed Cooks, Room service waiters, and construction workers of this hotel, who are native Maya people who work so cheaply at $3 a day with no other benefit. They are being treated poorly, and therefore, the author has set up equal work equal pay rights for the Maya Community and assigned attorneys to the work site for the development of human rights for laboring for them and the fund being paid by the Dumdeang Foundation.

Tulum Beach is well-known for its ancient Mayan ruins dating back to the 13th century. It is a perfect destination for historians and literature enthusiasts, located at the southernmost tip of the Riviera Maya. A 2-hour drive from Cancun, Tulum features beautiful beaches, crystal-clear waters, palm trees, and pristine golden-white sands. There are also stone-paved swimming pools nearby, making it an ideal place for swimming, along with several exciting beachfront hotels.

If you're looking for an escape from the hustle and bustle of the beach, Tulum offers the perfect retreat. The writer gathered relatives, friends, and children from both the United States and Thailand to host a grand wedding for Donna, the eldest daughter, in 2560, as previously described.

Due to language and cultural misunderstandings, many people mistakenly believe that the island is only for women (Woman Island). Even the writer initially thought so. However, upon visiting, the writer observed that most tourists were men who had traveled from all over the world.

The writer thanks the Thai Rath newspaper for clearly explaining the story of the city of Bahl, Mol.

The ancient Mayans were more ruthless than we ever knew!

(Thai Rath Online, September 8, 2562)

The ancient Maya priests, dressed in their distinctive Quetzal feather attire, were preparing to plunge a stone blade into the chest of a victim lying motionless on a stone altar atop a pyramid. Their aim was to extract the still-beating heart, which would be raised above the victim's head as a sacred offering to the gods. This grim and familiar image comes from the civilization of Mesoamerica, specifically ancient Mexico. However, in reality, such brutal heart-sacrifice rituals were more commonly associated with the Aztec people, who rose to power in the ancient Americas around the year 1300.

For another civilization that flourished in the nearby regions and also dominated the lands of Mexico, Guatemala, and Honduras.

And Belize, before that, was home to the ancient Maya civilization, which, unlike the Aztecs, had far fewer gruesome rituals. This has led archaeologists to suggest that the ancient Maya were significantly more "merciful" people compared to the Aztecs.

However, the latest discovery in early August 2019 seems to completely change the perspective on the gentleness of the ancient Maya. It now appears that the ancient Maya were not as "peaceful" or "gentle" as Mayan scholars once suggested. In addition, the ancient Maya engaged in "Total War," fighting with full force and using all available resources to annihilate their enemies. Surprisingly, the instigators of these wars may have been *women*!

The historical period of the ancient Maya civilization in which this discovery was made is known as the "Classic Period." This era flourished between **AD 250 and 900**, marking the peak of the ancient Maya city-states. However, by **AD 900**, these city-states mysteriously collapsed and disappeared without a trace.

Human sacrifice by heart extraction of the Aztecs

In the past, Mayan scholars proposed that the collapse of the ancient Maya civilization during the Classic period was due to climate change, leading to severe droughts that forced the Maya to engage in violent conflicts over food and resources. However, new evidence suggests that these ancient peoples may have clashed so intensely that they engaged in a "scorched-earth" strategy, burning down cities and settlements to the ground—even before the drought reached a critical level that would have necessitated fighting over food.

The protagonist cities of our story from the Classic period are two in number. The first is the city of **Naranjo**, located in eastern Guatemala, near the western border of Belize. The second city is **Witzna**, situated about 32 kilometers north of Naranjo.

What makes this archaeological discovery particularly fascinating is that the evidence uncovered at the excavation site in Witzna aligns perfectly with inscriptions carved into stone by the ancient Maya in Naranjo. The consistency between these two pieces of evidence strongly suggests that they describe the same historical event—the **great burning of Witzna**.

The inscription found on a stone stele in **Naranjo** contains records of wars between Naranjo and other city-states in the region. One particular passage has been translated as follows:

"On the day 3 Ben 16 Sek, the city of Bahlam Jol was burned for the second time."

This text mentions the date in the ancient Maya calendar system, which can be converted to May 21, 697 CE. This means that the second burning of "Bahlam Jol" took place during the Classic Period, which was the height of the ancient Maya civilization.

The next question is: where exactly was the city of "Bahlam Jol" located within the empire? This is not an easy question to answer. As we know, the ancient Maya civilization was an empire nestled deep within the jungle, more suited for adventurers like "Indiana Jones" than regular archaeologists. Moreover, the Maya civilization still has many areas hidden beneath the dense jungle that remain undiscovered. This makes the search for the city of "Bahlam Jol," based on inscriptions from the city of Naranjo, quite challenging. However, in this case, it's fortunate because Maya scholars have discovered another clue from the city of "Witzna," where the term "Bahlam Jol" appeared as a symbol representing the city. This indicates that "Bahlam Jol" and "Witzna" are actually the same city.

Additionally, an archaeological discovery from a depth of 7 meters beneath the lake, which dates back to the same period as the ancient Maya civilization, further supports the idea that the city "Bahlam Jol" mentioned in the ancient Maya inscriptions is the same as the city "Witzna" identified by modern Maya researchers. This discovery is in the area of the ancient city of Witzna, reinforcing the theory that both names refer to the same city.

Many of you may be familiar with the basic principle of archaeological excavation, where deeper layers of soil usually indicate older periods compared to those closer to the surface (although this can vary depending on other factors). Using this principle, archaeologists can analyze what happened in the past by drilling into the layers of lake sediments and collecting samples from different depths to examine. The results have been quite surprising. The sediment layers in the lake of the city of Witzna have accumulated rapidly, with an accumulation rate of about one centimeter per year, suggesting that the ancient Maya in this area had a significant impact.

The deforestation, which could have involved clearing land for agricultural purposes, is evident. Pollen grains of corn found in various sediment layers suggest that the ancient Maya likely used this area for farming activities. This indicates that agriculture was an important aspect of life for the ancient Maya in this region.

The captives who were captured by the ancient Maya kings had blood flowing from the tips of their fingers.

Another observation made by archaeologists from the evidence they examined was the layer of soil about 3 centimeters thick, compressed with charcoal. While clearing and burning forests to prepare agricultural land was a regular practice for the ancient Maya in the Classic period, the archaeologists examining the soil from the Witzna lakebed stated that they had never seen such a thick 3-centimeter layer of charcoal before. Therefore, it is unlikely that this came from the usual forest clearing. Additionally, another piece of evidence found in the upper soil layers above the thick charcoal layer showed that the pollen of maize decreased unusually. Before archaeologists could draw conclusions, the questions that needed to be answered were...

The next question is when exactly did this thick layer of charcoal form?

One of the reliable methods for dating in archaeology is using Carbon-14 dating. Fortunately, we have charcoal evidence that contains carbon, making this process feasible. The results indicate that the thick layer of charcoal formed between the years 690 and 700 AD, which corresponds to the peak period of the Classic Maya civilization. Additionally, no evidence of drought has been found during this time. Meanwhile, the layer of soil that contains corn pollen, which showed a significant reduction, suggests that this phenomenon occurred several centuries later, aligning with other evidence indicating a drought during the decline of the Classic Maya civilization.

But does the period from the carbon-14 testing results seem familiar?

The stone tablet from the city of Naranjo, which is presented as containing an inscription about the city of Bahlam Jo

The inscription from the city of Naranjo states that the city of "Bahlam Jol" was burned for the second time in the year 697 AD. Additionally, evidence has been found of symbols indicating that Bahlam Jol is the same as the city of Witzna. These two pieces of evidence led archaeologists to hypothesize that "Bahlam Jol" must be the same place as "Witzna," which has evidence of a 3-centimeter-thick layer of charcoal. This supports the idea that the city of Witzna, or Bahlam Jol, was indeed "burned" on a large scale in the past, which aligns perfectly with the information on the stone tablet from the city of Naranjo.

The next question is, what new perspectives has the discovery of evidence related to the large-scale burning in the city of Vitsiná provided for archaeologists?

The army of ancient Maya.

Initially, scholars of Maya archaeology suggested that the cause of the collapse of the ancient Maya civilization in the Classic period around 900 AD was due to droughts that led to food shortages. This event triggered the once peaceful Maya people to engage in wars, fighting each other over resources, leading to the destruction of several cities. However, the discovery of evidence in the city of Witzna has caused Maya scholars to reassess this theory. Although the ancient Maya did engage in battles for territory, capture of kings for ransom, or taking prisoners for sacrifice, scholars now propose that these conflicts were ceremonial wars to demonstrate power and grandeur, not wars of destruction. There is no evidence of a "destructive" war that would have leveled cities with large-scale "city burning" until this discovery.

The 6 Celestial Queens of the Naranho Kingdom

This means that the war between the Naranho kingdom and the city of Witsna in 697 AD was no longer merely a ritualistic war. Instead, it became a "total war," where the invader's goal was to "destroy" all of the enemy's forces, including people, homes, and agricultural land. This shows that the ancient Maya (at certain points in history) were far more brutal and "war-hungry" than previously suggested by scholars. Another point that needs to be reconsidered is that the drought was not the direct trigger for the wars between the cities, which ultimately led to the collapse of the ancient Maya civilization in 900 AD. The wars actually started before the drought played a role in the late classic period of the ancient Maya civilization, which lasted for several centuries.

Moreover, we also see that the one who initiated this brutal war was not a man but a "woman." According to the history of the Naranho kingdom, during the time of the great city burning in Witsna, the ruler of Naranho was a "queen" named "Lady 6 Sky." She tried to restore her dynasty, which was in decline, to its former glory by waging war against all the surrounding city-states that attempted to resist.

Mayan researchers have learned that, in addition to Witsna, the same Naranho stone also mentions three other cities that were "burned" violently in the same war. Although the destruction of the city in such a brutal manner did not immediately lead to the complete downfall of Witsna, this event allows us to imagine that when a "Mayan woman" rises to fight, she is ready to wage war with a level of "cruelty" that surpasses that of any man.

The writer's memoir.

Following the dream, the writer visited Cancun Beach and Tulum Beach in Mexico with their wife on March 29, 2006.

Mario asked the writer yesterday why they chose Cancun Beach and why not another place. The writer responded that when they were a manager at Thunderbird Hotel, one of their younger relatives asked for help to increase his working hours. The writer asked him why.

He replied to the writer that he wanted to earn more money to have the opportunity to visit Cancun Beach, Mexico. The writer responded that Cancun Beach had been a long-time dream of theirs as well, and it was a dream for both the writer and their wife.

However, the writer didn't have enough time to take her to other parts of the world. Therefore, the writer told him that Cancun, especially Chichen Itza, a place of interest, was the main goal. Except for the fact that the writer had time to visit the Taj Mahal in India or travel to Greece.

That was the answer the writer gave to his younger sibling. He felt very pleased when the writer said, "On the way back, don't forget to bring back some beautiful special photos for me."

Time passed, and one day, probably in 2004, we went to book tickets at the airline agent. The writer said to his wife, "We will go on our honeymoon to Cancun, Mexico." She was so surprised and couldn't believe her ears because the writer had always dreamed of taking his wife to visit historical cities. He has long been interested in the culture of the Maya people and their historical sites, just as much as he is interested in the history and culture of ancient Thailand.

Since the Sukhothai period up to the Ayutthaya period, it has always been in the writer's mind why it is similar to the pyramids in Egypt.

One week later, after we rushed to pick up our travel tickets from the agency in the city center, my wife received a lot of information from the library, which was kindly provided by a lady from the agency (please refer to the travel journal I had written earlier).

And one day, I remember it was in 2006, we flew to Cancun, Mexico, with a layover in Texas, USA. When we arrived in Cancun, Patty, my wife, felt that the atmosphere of the airport and the people was similar to Thailand, as their people still had low incomes, and the immigration officers lacked experience in their work. The problem was that the immigration officer said I was Thai, and since I was holding an American passport, I was told I needed a visa to enter Mexico. My wife argued that Dr. Sompong Damdaeng was holding an American passport and was an American citizen, so a visa was unnecessary. The officer continued to ask, "So, are you an immigrant to the United States?" I felt a little upset and replied, "Maybe, but do you know, I've done far more than you, someone who should be doing this job, but you haven't." The young immigration officer then asked for advice from his supervisor, who also had an American passport and didn't see the need for a visa. After that, I was allowed to enter Cancun.

A limousine took us to the hotel in Cancun. After that, we relaxed at the hotel, and the next day, we had a great time enjoying the atmosphere, delighting in various dishes, and eating everything we liked. We also booked tickets to visit nearby islands, such as Woman Island, and made arrangements to visit other attractions.

We visited several historical sites, making the most of our limited time with energy and enthusiasm. We learned how to utilize our time effectively, saving both time and money. We felt connected to the people around us, enjoying the experience with strength and vitality, as my wife had done before. We went to many places, enjoying both the natural beauty and human-made wonders, including Chichén Itzá, where most people gathered. The weather was scorching hot, so we left the group and enjoyed some cocoa before we had to stand in a long line under the heat. To cool off, we drank Coke, which made us feel a bit refreshed. Some American women seemed envious when they saw us having fun together. I jumped and swam in the pool, and one of the women asked if we had any aspirin, suggesting that it might help us avoid turning red from the heat. She made us realize a lot about ourselves, offering us aspirin while noticing our happiness. We spent the day swimming and enjoying each other's company.

We traveled to downtown by taking the local bus in Cancun, which arrived every 5 minutes. We made the most of our time in the city center, except that I didn't go to Munundo. We spent some time shopping at large stores like Walmart, among others.

When we were traveling to Chenshi, the bus broke down on the way. We were worried that there might be a robbery along the route. The writer focused and made a resolve in their mind that if a robbery actually happened, they would protect their wife and passengers with their lives. Of course, the Thai boxing skills learned from a former Thai boxing champion, a local from the south, would definitely be put to use if needed. Luckily, the driver quickly tried to make up for lost time, driving the bus as fast as possible to reach the destination with great anxiety. The writer shouted out loud...

He was still angry... "Stop, stop!" This is driving way too fast and is very dangerous for all of us on the bus. Everyone on the bus could see it, just like the writer. We decided to switch to another bus, and it took us safely to our destination.

The writer and his wife enjoy and are interested in visiting pyramids and learning about historical events. One such event is the history and culture of the Maya people. The writer is an expert in the history of minority groups, having researched and written articles about minorities both in Thailand and other countries in Asia, as well as in America. The writer's wife enjoys taking beautiful pictures, many of which were taken with the Maya people. This reminds the writer of his time teaching at a high school in America, David Daugus. We ate Maya dishes with excitement and took photos of historical sites with them as memories... it was very beautiful.

The traditional dances of the Maya people are similar to those of the hill tribes in northern Thailand, such as the dances of the Hmong people. We watched the dance with great interest. We booked seats on the lower level and bought drinks and food for our children.

Spanish

Spanish (español) or Castilian (Castellano) is a language in the Romance language group, one of the six official languages of the United Nations. It is the second most spoken native language in the world, after Mandarin Chinese. It is also the official language of several important international organizations in the fields of economics and politics, including the European Union, the African Union, the Organization of American States, the Ibero-American States Organization, the North American Free Trade Agreement, and the Union of South American Nations, among others.

There are between 450-500 million people who speak Spanish as their first or second language, with Mexico being the country with the highest number of speakers. Additionally, Spanish is the second most learned language in the world, after English, with at least 17.8 million learners. Some sources say that over 46 million people are learning the language across 90 countries. Spanish originates from the Latin language of the Iberian Peninsula, which developed in the 3rd century AD (like other languages in the Romance language group). After the fall of the Roman Empire, the territories that were once part of the empire became separate and governed by various groups. As a result, the language was cut off from the Latin dialects of other regions and slowly evolved into a distinct new Latin language. However, due to its spread across North and South America, the language continued to thrive.

Spanish is one of the languages that the writer likes because its grammar has similarities with Pali and Sanskrit, which are ancient languages of India. These languages play a significant role in the teachings of Buddhism, especially Pali. The writer has studied and learned about the curriculum for teaching Pali, which is used by monks who have completed their studies.

The highest level of Buddhist studies is the Nine Levels of Dhamma, which the writer has studied for a long time. As for Sanskrit, the writer studied it at the Buddhist University of Thailand, Mahachulalongkornrajavidyalaya, and continued their studies at Banaras Hindu University in India.

- Hispanic-American Indians
- Latin American Indians
- Mayas
- Toitec
- Aztecs
- Incas
- Other Cannibalism
- Skull Hunters

The Aztec Calendar is not just an ordinary calendar; it is a calendar used to explain the relationship between the universe, the movement of time, and the stars. This calendar was used by the ancient Aztecs, similar to other cultures in central Mexico. It is one of the calendars of the Mesoamerican peoples, which share a common structure for their calendars, originating from ancient Mesoamerica. The Aztec sunstone, or the Aztec calendar, is displayed in the National Museum of Anthropology in Mexico City.

Mexico City has a unique carved stone with a diameter of 12 feet and weighs 12,000 pounds, known as the "Stone of the Sun" or the Aztec Sun Stone. This stone is highly accurate as it represents a model of the universe, encompassing five eras of the sun and the cosmos. It is an important cultural artifact that showcases the Aztecs' deep understanding of time and the universe.

The Aztec Sun Stone features seven concentric circles. The second circle depicts the four ways the world was destroyed by different forces: monstrous creatures, winds, storms, and floods. The first circle illustrates the Sun's appearance, symbolizing the need for human blood and sacrifice. The remaining five circles represent the paths of the stars, and the last circle shows two mythical serpents whose tails meet at the top, symbolizing a cosmic event or transformation in Aztec cosmology.

Latin American Indians

Indigenous people from Mexico, Central America, and South America have lived on this continent for over 5,000 years. There are more than 51 tribes and over 30 spoken languages.

These indigenous people are hardworking, love their families, and are deeply connected to their communities. They are joyful, sing songs, and dance beautifully in celebration of festivals dedicated to the gods, enjoying themselves in the process.

Approximately 25 million indigenous people still live according to ancient traditions, blending them with Christianity.

Their religious perspective is related to the concept of being animals, with their beliefs connected to spirituality.

They worship the Sun, the Moon, and strange animals and often consider the emperor himself to be a god.

Belief in multiple gods is strictly forbidden in the scriptures, as there is only one God. Anything else is considered to be the work of demons.

The scriptures condemn all forms of astrology and divination.

The Bible condemns all forms of astrology, prophecy, magic, demons, witches, and belief in spirits and deities, etc.

The scripture states, "It is an abomination to the Lord" and "To throw stones to have them die" (Deuteronomy 18, Leviticus 20) because placing trust and offering oneself to idols or other gods is compared to a wife giving herself to another man who is not her husband. The sin of idol worship is called prostitution in the Bible, a direct act of defiance against God, and is considered a great sin (Lev. 20).

Indian culture has received high praise, and in Mexico alone, there have been excavations of up to 13,000 archaeological sites.

Mayas

The Maya people have lived in Guatemala and Mexico for about 3,000 years. Their central ceremonial center disappeared completely around 869 BC, and the cause remains unknown.

The capital is located in Guatemala, while Palenque in Yucatan is one of the most beautiful and stunning places. Nearby Mexico City, the city of Teotihuacan is a ceremonial center and a famous city known worldwide. It is home to two Indian pyramids, and discoveries have shown that the walls were decorated with intricate murals.

The pyramids in this region are different from those in Egypt, as the pyramids in Egypt serve as tombs for the deceased. However, in the Maya cities, the pyramids are central locations for rituals, serving as places of worship and sacrifice to the gods. The rituals often involved the removal of the hearts of virgin women as offerings.

Some of their gods, such as "Itzamna," are considered to represent the highest form of life. He is the god of fire and also the deity associated with the heart of the feathered serpent Kukulcán. The god K has a baroque-like appearance, with branching nostrils, and holds a staff in the hand of the ceremonial leader.

Toltecs

In 975 AD, Toltec warriors migrated to the city of Tula, near Mexico City and Veracruz. After defeating the Maya, they established themselves in Yucatán and at Chichen Itza, which became the central ceremonial site of the Maya. They settled in Mayapan in 987 and in Uxmal in 1007.

They practiced human sacrifice through the method of tzompantli, where skulls were displayed on racks as a symbol of death.

The Aztecs came from Aztlan (the land of whiteness, located in the north of Mexico in the 12th century). They were known as Tenocha and Mexica, originating from Metzilapan (the lake of the moon). Tenocha became their capital city, known as Tenochtitlan, which is now present-day Mexico.

The last leader of the Aztecs, Montezuma, was killed in 1521. After that, the Aztec Empire was conquered by Spain under the leadership of Hernán Cortés.

The pyramid, which resembles a temple to the Aztec gods, was located in the city of Tenochtitlan. Each year, about 20,000 people were sacrificed to the Aztec gods, especially to Huizilopochtli, the god of the sun and war. The hearts of the humans were torn out and offered to the gods.

The Aztecs believed that as a people, they had a sacred responsibility to prevent the destruction of the world during the fifth era, following four previous destructions caused by the death of the sun and wars. To prevent a new catastrophe, they believed they had to sustain the sun with human hearts and blood.

The Aztec religion emphasized sacrifice and ascetic behaviors, which were considered essential conditions for approaching the divine and spiritual matters beyond.

Above nature, the ascetic will be honored and celebrated, living a simple Spartan life by performing ascetic practices through threading strings through the ears.

The Aztec approach to contacting the supernatural was through a complex, layered ritual that would take place at temples, conducted by ascetics who served as intermediaries between the gods and humans. Throughout these ceremonies, human hearts were sacrificed to gain favor from the gods. In dreams, theatrical performances, which included dancing, wearing masks, singing, and parading the Earth deity, were prominent, and there were many gods involved.:

The Aztec religion centered around the sun, but Tlaloc, the god of rain, held equal stature to the sun god. After death, good deeds would lead to heaven, while evil deeds would result in a dark and cold descent into hell.

Inca religion was a fusion of complex rituals, beliefs in superstition and spirits in various forms (belief in objects with special powers), and the worship of nature, culminating in the worship of the sun god.

The ascetics would offer rituals, mostly consisting of white llamas and coca leaves. They would call upon spirits to communicate by chanting 'fire' as a way to connect spiritually before performing any rituals. Divination was similar to that of the Romans, with basic practices such as arranging coca leaves, using coca leaves as medicine, and studying the lungs of sacrificial priests.

Humans still sacrificed young children, up to 200 people, often by beating them to death. When Sapa Inca took power after being defeated by famine and plague, all were in search of human blood.

Women who were chosen had to swear an oath of perpetual virginity and austerity. Upon death, those who had lived virtuously—' not stealing, not lying, not being lazy'—would enter an eternal peaceful world.

Other Latin American Indians in Paraguay.

The Jesuit Order, arriving from Spain, established missionary groups among them, forcing them to cease warfare and stop eating human flesh. The modern population of Paraguay descends from these Native Americans, and even today, they can still speak the Guaraní language.

The Native Americans in Chile, the Araucanians, resisted Spanish colonization and maintained their unity throughout the colonial era. However, when Chile gained independence, the Araucanians became citizens of Chile.

Native Americans in Argentina.

The Puelche tribe of the Pampas learned to ride horses, which were introduced by the Spanish. The Puelche tribe became formidable warriors, such as the famous Cammineche and Ceuks of the North American plains.

Native Americans in Colombia and Central America.

The Chibehan tribe of Native Americans would often leave diamonds and gold with their tribal chiefs, believing that after death, they would go to a better place. Robbing the graves of these Native American tribes became a common practice, continuing for many centuries. It seems that in Colombia, there were brutal wars fought to capture prisoners for consumption and sacrifice.

Native Americans in the Caribbean and Brazil.

Native Americans in the Caribbean and Brazil are not very well-known, but they are recognized to some extent.

Regarding the religions brought by slaves from African countries, most of them reside in Santería,

104

Paloma Mayo, and Abakíw in Cuba. The Vodou in Haiti, the Macumba, the Candomblé, and the Umbanda in Brazil have been discussed in relation to the religions of Africa.

Cannibalism

When the Spanish and Portuguese arrived in the Americas, they discovered that there were many instances of cannibalism and headhunting. Most of these practices were found in forested areas. The Spanish referred to the cannibalistic practices in the New World as cannibalism. The reason they practiced cannibalism was to gain strength by eating fresh human flesh. Missionaries were the group that fought to abolish cannibalism and imposed strict prohibitions against it.

Reports indicate that all ethnic groups in the temperate zone and the Arctic region have connections to beliefs in sorcery and religious practices. In Western Africa, consuming death was considered an honor. Eating fresh human flesh was regarded as a ritual to ensure success in trade. In Melanesia, death was consumed to take on the spiritual power of the deceased. However, in Australia and Polynesia, human flesh was considered a revered food and viewed as something repulsive.

Skull Hunters

Headhunters would reduce the size of the skull to the size of a fist, then hang it at the front of their houses as a war trophy. Most of these can be found in museums in New York City.

Chapter 10

Visiting Rome

Beliefs and faiths in one's own religion often share similarities. For example, Buddhists often have a desire to visit important Buddhist sites in India, such as the places of birth, enlightenment, and parinirvana of the Buddha, the founder of Buddhism. As the writer's teacher, Ajahn Maha Phrom Pimiyathammo, once said, 'Before there is no life, I wish to have the opportunity to visit the places of the Buddha's birth, enlightenment, and parinirvana.' The writer was able to fulfill this wish by taking the teacher to visit those places in India during the time when the writer was studying in India, which brought great joy to the teacher.

While Muslims also wish to have the opportunity to make a pilgrimage to the city of Mecca, Saudi Arabia, at least once in their lifetime, it is evident that each year, millions of Muslims from around the world travel to Mecca for the pilgrimage.

Meanwhile, every Christian longs to visit the cathedral in Rome, Italy, during their lifetime. The wife of the author is a devout Christian, and her family has long been a patron of the church. She often mentioned to the author that she wished to have the opportunity to make a pilgrimage to Rome, visit the cathedral, and see the residence of the Pope. Rome itself is also the center of Western civilization. Therefore, the author decided to fulfill his wife's wish. The author also considered it a blessing in life to have the chance to visit Rome and, if fortunate, receive a blessing from the Pope. Hence, the author decided to take his wife to Rome, Italy.

Every time the author travels abroad, whether it's to Asia, the Caribbean, Jamaica, Latin America, or Europe, the author and their family, relatives, and friends always use the services of Cathy Farn, a reliable travel agent who provides excellent services through the Horizon Travellers Account. She arranges everything comprehensively, including taxi services to pick up from airports around the world. Whether the author is traveling by train, staying at hotels, or using her services, there has never been any disappointment. For this trip to Rome, the author had her arrange the flight tickets, taxis, hotel accommodations, and train services.

The author and his wife traveled from Portland to Texas, then to Germany, and finally arrived in Rome. The journey took a long time. When they reached Rome, a taxi with a personal sign reading

'Welcome Patty Dumdeang' was waiting to pick them up. This was arranged to honor the author's wife, making Patty very surprised as the welcome sign only had her name. Their entry into Europe went smoothly. Upon arrival, the first view was unforgettable. The first-class Mercedes-Benz taxi took them to the heart of Rome. The author felt that the city's layout was somewhat similar to Sampeng in their hometown—narrow streets with no parking spaces, and both entrances and alleys were very tight. They stayed at the Albani Roma Hotel (www.albanihotel.com).

The hotel manager's hospitality was excellent, and the welcome for both of us was outstanding. However, it was noticeable that some parts of the hotel were under repair and renovation. We were taken to a first-class suite, as per our reservation. This hotel is considered a central hub for everything—bars, restaurants, shopping, and more—similar to a high-end hotel located in the middle of a business district, offering all services to guests from around the world.

The next morning at breakfast, Patty asked the writer why children aged 6-8-10 were dressed neatly, wearing white shirts, neat trousers, and ties while sitting in the dining room. The writer replied that it is a European tradition, especially in Italy. They often dress like the upper class because they consider themselves the rightful owners of the land and of civilized culture. Patty always pays attention to details about the customs and traditions of the countries she visits. This is her natural characteristic, as she has been a professor at a university in America for no less than 25 years, and her students come from all over the world.

The restaurant of the hotel is spacious and luxurious, and has a very inviting atmosphere. The Italian-style food, including soft-boiled and hard-boiled eggs, prepared by world-class chefs, is a favorite of the writer's wife. It has become her regular habit. The writer himself enjoys Italian food very much, and since he loves cooking, he has also brought Italian cooking methods to America.

The writer and his wife joined the hotel's tour bus after receiving advice from the hotel's service department. The hotel's bus would take guests staying at the hotel on a sightseeing tour to important places in Rome along a designated route, as well as to places the passengers wanted to visit. It was a convenient and cost-effective option compared to using a private taxi. Taking this opportunity to gain more experience, they decided to join the hotel's tour bus.

The first stop the bus took us to was St. Peter's Square. This place is the central point for everything, with a vast area much larger than the Emerald Buddha Temple in our country. The writer and his wife got lost several times, and the guide had to look for them. However, they spent the entire day there.

We found a way to meet the Pope.

During the writer's visit to Rome it happened to coincide with the Christmas season, so there were tourists from all over the world traveling to Rome to meet the Pope, just like the writer and his wife. We had to stand in a long queue with thousands of people who were also hoping to meet the Pope. The Vatican Security Officer approached the writer and asked, "Are you from Thailand?" Perhaps the officer had previously served Thai tourists or was familiar with Thai people. Upon seeing the writer, the officer immediately assumed he was Thai. The writer replied politely that he was not from Thailand but from America. The writer took the opportunity to introduce his wife, Patty Dumdeang, and mentioned that it was her dream to meet the Pope, which she had wanted since she was a young girl in America. The officer appeared to be very friendly, and the writer asked if he had ever visited America. The officer quickly replied, "Not yet, but I would love to visit." The writer immediately offered to help if the officer ever visited America, offering a place to stay and a tour guide, as well as assistance with housework since they had a property rental business in America. The officer, in return, helped the writer and his wife by bypassing the long queue to meet the Pope immediately. The writer and his wife were grateful, and they expressed their thanks to the officer for his kind assistance.

The Pope's security officer introduced the writer and his wife to the Pope, saying, "Your Holiness, these two are Dr. Sompong Dumdeang and Madam Dumdeang from the United States of America. They are your special guests. Both of them have long had a strong desire and dream since their youth to have the opportunity to meet Your Holiness in person during their lifetime…

The Pope replied, "Thank you very much.

After bidding farewell to the Pope, the two of us spent time admiring the world-renowned artwork in the Sistine Chapel, from the ceiling down to the floor. The ceiling paintings created by Michelangelo especially captivated my wife. She was particularly drawn to the image of the Virgin Mary giving birth to Jesus. She spent more time studying and reading about this scene than the others. Once we finished viewing the various pieces of art, we met with the master and sister from the souvenir department. We purchased books, various types of coins, and prints of Jesus' images to bring back as gifts for my mother-in-law, as well as other items, including small wooden souvenirs for our family and friends back in America.

Afterward, we returned to the hotel by taxi because we had arrived later than expected. The hotel tour bus had already departed hours earlier. That evening, we went for a short sightseeing trip near the hotel. We asked the concierge for recommendations on the best restaurants in the area. We received excellent suggestions and were not disappointed. We went to one of the recommended restaurants, which made me feel as though we were in Thailand, as we enjoyed a wonderful Italian seafood dinner.

In Italian restaurants, the dining table is set with four glasses per person: one for water, one for white wine or liquor, one for red wine, and one for soda. This is part of Italian dining culture, as Italians enjoy pairing wine with their meals. The staff offered us wine, but if we declined, they were respectful and did not insist. This is a tradition in Italy.

The Italian restaurant served delicious food, and I was feeling quite hungry. The place was crowded with both Italians and tourists from all over the world. I planned to ask the restaurant owner to come over and serve us at our table. I spoke with the server and asked if they remembered me and my wife, but it seemed that they didn't recall us. Peter, who was very hungry, had gone to find another restaurant.

Peter replied, "Why not? I remember both of you very well." He then asked about the head chef and the kitchen staff. Within a minute, the head chef and all the kitchen staff came out to greet us, eagerly apologizing for not having served us earlier. It had been a while since we'd met. The head chef said, "Alright, everything tonight is on hold." His sincerity was beyond belief.

The plan worked even better than expected. In Thai, we would call this "a playful jest," and using humor with technique always produces great results. My hunger was the perfect excuse to use this approach, and it worked like a charm, leaving my wife puzzled. However, I didn't explain it to her until today, as it was just a technique of mine.

After we finished our meal and enjoyed the wine that perfectly suited our taste, we returned to the hotel and had a restful night's sleep.

Rome

Rome, or Roma in Italian, is the capital and largest city of the Lazio region and Italy. Located in the central part of the country, the city has a population of approximately 2.5 million people within the city limits. Including the surrounding areas, the population reaches around 4.3 million, making it comparable in size to Milan and Naples.

Additionally, Rome is also the location of Vatican City, which is the land where the headquarters of the Roman Catholic Church and the residence of the Pope are situated. Vatican City is an independent sovereign state, distinct from the city of Rome.

After the end of the Middle Ages, Rome was under the rule of the Papacy, such as Pope Alexander VI and Pope Leo X, who played a significant role in transforming Rome into one of the central hubs of the Italian Renaissance, alongside Florence. During this era, the construction of St. Peter's Basilica was initiated, as seen in its current form. Michelangelo also painted the Sistine Chapel ceiling. Famous artists and architects such as Bramante, Bernini, and Raphael, who lived in Rome temporarily, contributed to the development of Renaissance and Baroque architecture and art in the city.

In 2550, Rome was the 11th most visited city in the world, the third most visited in the European Union, and the most popular tourist destination in Italy. The historical center of the city has been listed as a UNESCO World Heritage site. Additionally, landmarks such as the Vatican Museums and the Colosseum are among the top 50 most visited tourist attractions in the world, with the Vatican Museums drawing 4.2 million visitors annually and the Colosseum attracting 4 million visitors each year.

Florence

Florence, or Firenze in Italian, is a city located in the central part of Italy. It is the capital and largest city of the Tuscany region. Florence has a population of 383,084 people, and when including the surrounding metropolitan area, the population reaches approximately 1.5 million.

Florence was a central hub for commerce and finance during the Middle Ages and was considered one of the wealthiest cities of that era. Many scholars regard Florence as the birthplace of the Renaissance, and it has been called the "Athens of the Middle Ages." The history of Florence is quite complex, from being ruled by the Medici family and the clergy to the revolutionary period that led to its status as a republic. Between 1865 and 1871, Florence served as the capital of the Kingdom of Italy (established in 1861). The Florentine dialect became the foundation of the standard Italian language, which is now spoken across all of Italy. These achievements are attributed to influential figures like Dante Alighieri, Petrarch, Giovanni Boccaccio, and Niccolò Machiavelli.

Florence attracts millions of tourists every year and was designated a UNESCO World Heritage site in 1982. The city is renowned for its rich culture, Renaissance architecture, and legendary artworks. Within the city, there are numerous galleries and museums, such as the Uffizi Gallery and the Pitti Palace. Florence is also an important hub for the Italian fashion industry, ranking as the 15th fashion capital of the world. Forbes magazine has ranked Florence among the most beautiful cities in the world.

In addition to traveling by airplane, most travelers in Europe use rental cars or trains. The writer didn't want to rent a car, so they booked a train ticket from Rome to Florence, a round trip. Despite having made the reservation in advance, the train station was packed, and the writer almost missed their train because they were helping an Indian ambassador who couldn't read Italian. The ambassador was also traveling to Florence with the writer. In Italy, they don't use English as a universal language; but instead, they use Italian as the official language. This could be due to the country's nationalism. The three of them— the writer, the writer's wife, and the Indian ambassador— were trying to find signs in English that indicated Rome and Florence, as the signs were written in Italian (Roma-Firenze), not in English (Rome-Florence), as English speakers would write them.

The train ride from Rome to Florence took about 4.5 hours. Of course, the scenery along the way was beautiful. We became acquainted with an American couple sitting on the same train. They were traveling to Venice and invited us to join them. However, the writer didn't feel it was convenient, so they declined the invitation. Patty felt that it would be too tiring to visit several cities within a limited time. Most importantly, Patty wanted to return to celebrate Christmas with her family in America. She had always dreamed of visiting Venice in her lifetime. The writer didn't want to go against her wishes and decided to postpone the trip to Venice for now.

We arrived in Florence around 1 AM that night. We checked into the Athens Hotel, which is located in the city center.

Florence is considered just as famous as Rome. However, Rome's significance mainly lies in being the seat of the Pope. When it comes to art, culture, traditions, lifestyle, and cuisine, Florence's vibrancy is on par with Rome, and the atmosphere here even seems to have an edge over Rome.

Patty's top priority was to visit an ancient Catholic church, which was also included in the itinerary for our tour of Florence. It's important to understand that Florence is a city full of museums—every building seems to house another museum. The city itself is paved with stone, and there's hardly any sandy ground to be seen. In Florence, there are no cars, and walking is the primary mode of transportation. When we asked the locals for directions to a museum, they would tell us it was "just a couple of blocks away." But in reality, it was more like 15-20 blocks away. It's similar to how we walked in Vancouver— both of us were used to walking like the locals in Florence. We spent half a day exploring one of the city's grand museums according to our agenda.

We walked around exploring the art and reading historical brochures. Patty, my wife, was particularly interested in the history of Native Americans in the Florence area, and she read about it enthusiastically.

I waited for her while observing the historical depiction of various Native American tribes. It made me reflect on how similar human existence is across the world. Whether it's the Native Americans in America, the Mexicans, or the tribes in the northern regions of Thailand—where I had once lived in remote areas of Phetchabun province—the differences between cultures seem to be far less significant than the similarities that unite us.

There are some similarities in terms of climate, and also in the way people live and sustain themselves. Eventually, we reached the meditation session—an area for the senior Catholic monks to practice meditation. I felt deeply moved to see the private rooms, each one meticulously clean and simple, designed to foster peace of mind for meditation. The rooms had small windows that let natural light shine in, creating a serene atmosphere.

We spent some time meditating in one of the rooms, and both Patty and I felt a sense of peace and clarity, similar to what one might experience meditating in the meditation hall at Suan Mokkh, the Buddhist temple in Chaiya, Surat Thani, Thailand. Afterward, we stepped outside to breathe in the fresh air, sitting in a car to admire the flowers and plants in the public garden in front of the museum.

The Galileo St. Thomas Augustin Museum, located in the northern part of Florence, is a place of great interest for the author, who is a philosophy professor with a deep admiration for Italian philosophy. As a result, the author decided to visit this museum. Within the museum, there is a tomb where many philosophers are buried, such as Galileo and St. Thomas. The author felt puzzled by the differences between Italian traditions and Thai customs. In Thailand, there is a cultural respect that prohibits stepping on the graves of notable individuals, which made the author curious about why the museum would display the remains of philosophers in a way where people walk over them, seemingly with no reverence. The notable figures in the museum include Donato Bramante, Michelangelo, Carlo Maderno, and Gian Lorenzo.

However, the author felt a great sense of pride in having visited these philosophers, just as Thai people often dream of visiting the birthplace, enlightenment, and parinirvana sites of the Buddha in India to pay their respects.

After that, we stood in line to buy dozens of types of candy to bring back as souvenirs for family and relatives in America. Shopping in Florence is a unique experience because the city offers products from all over the world, including well-known Italian silk, Italian wine, or Florence wines, handmade women's clothing, Florence candies, roasted pork, or roasted pork (similar to the grilled and roasted pork from Chiang Mai or Chiang Rai in northern Thailand).

The author bought several bottles of Florence wine and shipped them from Florence to Portland, America. The shop owner was a professor teaching at a university in Rome. We introduced ourselves to each other, which helped the author receive a 15% discount, partly because of the large quantity purchased and partly because we shared the same profession as university professors. The shop owner also informed the author that he had a wine distributor in Portland. These are the items the author bought as gifts for the family in America. Meanwhile, Patty bought several types of candy for the grandchildren and relatives in America, along with various works of art from Florence.

Chapter 11

Visiting Louisiana

Louisiana

Louisiana is located far from Portland, Oregon, USA, where the writer resides. The total distance is 3,107 kilometers or 1,931 miles. If traveling by car along Highway 1-84 west, the journey takes about 37 hours and 22 minutes.

Louisiana is a southern state of the United States with a blend of French culture. Both English and French are the official languages of the state. Although French is only used by about 5% of the population, it holds cultural significance. The most notable city in the state is New Orleans, which is the largest city in Louisiana, while the state capital is Baton Rouge. Famous sports teams in the state include the New Orleans Saints and the New Orleans Hornets.

In the past, Louisiana was part of the French colony of Louisiana. The U.S. government made a purchase agreement with Napoleon Bonaparte in 2346, acquiring this territory. The state's name, "Louisiana," comes from King Louis XIV of France, meaning "Land of Louis."

In 2550, Louisiana had a population of 4,089,963 people. Every year, a large celebration called Mardi Gras is held in New Orleans. The event includes parades and various festive activities, typically taking place in late February or early March.

In 2548, Hurricane Katrina caused severe damage, especially in New Orleans. It was a tremendous loss for the people of Louisiana. At that time, the U.S. government declared a state of emergency to provide aid to those affected by the natural disaster, an event that had never occurred before in America.

While working at the Teknomix factory in Memberton, Oregon, which is a high-tech electronics manufacturing plant with a global export market, the writer held a managerial position at level 3. This was during the first wave of Asian immigrants arriving in the United States as a result of the Vietnam War, with the initial wave beginning in 1980. At that time, the writer kept in regular contact with their brother, Phichin, who was a judge for the Labor Court in Thailand. Phichin informed the writer that he would be traveling to the U.S. to attend an international labor relations conference hosted by the United States. As a leader in Thai labor, Phichin was invited by the U.S. government to attend the conference.

The writer did not receive a definite travel schedule from Phichin, making it impossible to arrange their own activities until Phichin's arrival, as they were eagerly waiting to welcome him. This was particularly important since the two had a long-standing close relationship, dating back to their time as novice monks together in Songkhla, southern Thailand.

Thai Labor Movement during 1978-1980

The significance of the issue and the concept of labor unions as a social movement (Social movement unionism) began to appear in the works of Western scholars from the mid-1980s onwards (such as the works of Touraine 1986, Munck 1988, and Waterman 1993). After explaining the role of labor unions worldwide according to the Marxist theory of class struggle, some scholars pointed out that the labor movement led by unions has evolved and changed. It now shares characteristics with the new social movement (New social movement).

For example, labor unions in the Third World countries, such as Brazil, South Africa, India, and Poland, have played a role in fighting for the interests of workers who are not union members. These unions have also collaborated with other social movements in supporting each other's causes (Munck, 1988: 106).

In the past, the Thai labor movement was characterized as a social movement that often collaborated with other movements focusing on social and political issues. This began during the pre-revolutionary period before the 2475 political change and continued with a clear role in social movements following the October 14, 2516 events, until the 2519 military coup, or the May. 2535 demonstrations, and the movement advocating for the 2540 Constitution.

However, at certain points, labor movements with unions as the leading organizations were criticized for straying from being a social movement. This was because they focused solely on issues that directly benefited workers and neglected to participate in other movements addressing broader social issues. In the last decade, there has been a debate regarding the concept of unions as social movement organizations (Social movement unionism) in terms of practical implementation. However, there has yet to be a clear, shared understanding of this concept, including the analysis of whether such an approach could be a viable option for the development of the Thai labor movement under the complex circumstances of global capitalism. This research project aims to find answers to this question.

Research Question

Main Question

How should the development of the Thai labor movement in the present, under the concept of labor unions as a social movement, be approached?

Sub-Questions

1. How has the concept of labor unions as a social movement evolved in the global context?

2. In the past, was the Thai labor movement considered a social movement? If so, in what way?

3. Can the current Thai labor movement develop into a social movement? If so, how?

Objective

1. To study the development approach of the Thai labor movement in the present under the concept of a labor union as a social movement.

2. To study the origin of the concept of a labor union as a social movement in the global context.

3. To study the social movement aspect of the Thai labor movement in the past.

4. To study the development toward becoming a social movement of the Thai labor movement in the present.

Research Methodology

1. The research adopts a qualitative approach with the following methods of data collection:

Document study related to the topic.

2. **Collecting and synthesizing opinions from labor leaders, leaders, and practitioners in other social movements, as well as scholars, by organizing discussion forums for brainstorming.**

3. **Conducting in-depth interviews or focus group discussions with labor leaders, leaders, and practitioners in other social movements, as well as scholars.**

4. **Timeframe for the study and report preparation**

The study and report preparation will take 10 months, from March to December 2017.

Expected outcomes:

1. The Thai labor movement will have a platform and data for reviewing its past and present roles in order to move toward developing itself as a social movement in the future.

2. The creation of academic knowledge to support collaboration in the civil sector between labor unions, civil society organizations, and scholars.

Chin Thongmee played a significant role in labor in Thailand during that period. He was chosen by the Thai labor union to be the labor leader of Thailand. Later, he was appointed as an associate judge for the Thai labor court and was invited by the U.S. government to serve as the host for the World Labor Union meeting held in St. Louis, New Orleans, United States.

Upon receiving the news via phone, Chin informed me that he had arrived in St. Louis, New Orleans, and was staying at the Hilton Hotel in the city center. At that time, it was just starting to approach winter, around October-November 1979. However, Chin probably remembers better than I do the exact day and month of his arrival. This coincided with the period of the U.S. presidential election campaign. The most popular candidate at the time was Ronald Reagan, the former Governor of California and a former famous Hollywood actor. I received a letter from the Governor of Oregon stating that, as a manager at the 3rd level of TechMix Corporation, along with my employer, Mr. John Meagapan, they requested that I be their representative.

The company acted as the representative in organizing a suitable venue to welcome the presidential candidates for the election, ensuring it was appropriate for their visit to the company.

The writer earned the high trust of the employer, who spoke with the writer, saying, "We trust you completely because you have taken care of many thousands of Asian immigrants who have come to live in America, and many of those who work with our company are also of Asian descent, making up about one-third of the immigrant population. He assigned the writer the task of representing the company in welcoming Ronald Reagan because he had confidence in the writer's ability to manage the workers and ensure they were ready to welcome Reagan well, given that the writer was close to and engaged with laborers, most of whom were of Asian descent.

Nevertheless, the writer still felt concerned. If the writer's brother had come to America at that time, the assigned task might become complicated because the writer was required to be fully prepared to take care of his brother, who was coming from Thailand. Therefore, the writer spoke with Mr. John, saying, "I will carry out the assigned task to the best of my ability, but if my senior friend comes to attend the meeting in America at that time, I will absolutely need to look after him as best as possible. The supervisor should take over the task." Mr. John understood the writer's situation, and we worked together on this.

It was a fortunate thing for the company to have an excellent manager like John. The company's administration progressed very well because John had previously lived in Thailand, served as a soldier in the Vietnam War, and had an adopted Cambodian child. He loved Thailand. As for the writer, the writer is Thai but studied at a leading university in America, and the writer's wife is American. This shared background allowed both of us to understand the cultures of labor and society from both sides, which helped the administration run smoothly. We were able to assist both Asian immigrants and local Americans well. It was also a stroke of luck that the reception for Ronald Reagan's campaign was successful before the writer's brother arrived.

When the writer's brother called to inform that he had arrived in St. Louis and was staying at the Hilton Hotel in downtown St. Louis, the writer asked for permission from John to travel immediately to meet him. The writer submitted a leave request for another week. John was initially reluctant to approve the leave at that time because it was a very busy period for the company. The company had a contract to deliver electronic equipment to NASA, with a value of several million dollars, and they had to expedite the work to deliver the products on time according to the contract. This would also help build trust with the client, which would serve as a guarantee for future cooperation. John said that if the writer's brother wasn't a relative and hadn't come from Thailand, he definitely wouldn't have allowed the leave.

The writer understood the responsibility and respected the boss's position, but the deep affection and bond that the writer had for their brother, who was still unfamiliar with the United States, led the writer to decide to meet the brother in St. Louis, Louisiana. Despite the distance of 3,107 kilometers from Portland, Oregon, where the writer lived, to St. Louis, it did not pose an obstacle to the journey.

The writer stayed at a 3-star hotel to save on expenses. Since the writer had not received confirmation from the brother about staying at the Hilton Hotel, the writer checked with the front desk of the Hilton Group Hotel. It was found that no reservation under the name "Mr. Chin Thongmee" from Thailand was listed. However, the writer did not give up and stayed in the downtown hotel for a week, attempting to find the brother. Unfortunately, the writer could not locate the brother at the international labor leader seminar that took place during that time. The writer then returned to Portland with a sense of disappointment and later learned that...

The main reason we were unable to meet on that occasion was due to the interpreter provided by the U.S. government for P'Chin. That interpreter may not have had enough experience because, when registering at the hotel, they used their own name instead of listing **Chin Thongmee from Thailand** as the guest. Therefore, it was impossible to check hotel records for P'Chin's name to locate him.

At an international seminar, participants from all over the world typically attend, and English is generally used as the official language. However, attendees from various countries often face language barriers. Therefore, the host provides interpreters to help participants understand the seminar content.

It was truly unfortunate for P'Chin to miss such an opportunity. If I had been his interpreter at that event, I could have assisted him effectively. I have extensive experience as a **Legal Interpreter** in the U.S. and a deep understanding of both Thai and American languages and culture. Additionally, I am certified as an interpreter by the U.S. Supreme Court.

I strongly believe that if I had been P'Chin's interpreter for that seminar, he would have benefited far more from the discussions. That was a missed opportunity indeed...

Later, Chin Thongmee resigned from his position as a Thai labor leader and also stepped down as an associate labor judge. He then immigrated to the United States, following in my footsteps. He got married and has lived there for over 30 years. He has since obtained U.S. citizenship legally.

This is the deep and long-lasting bond of love and connection between the writer and Chin Thongmee.

Chapter 12

A Visit to Arizona

State of Arizona

Arizona is a state in the southwestern region of the United States. It is the 6th largest state by area and the 14th most populous among the 50 states. The capital and largest city of Arizona is Phoenix.

Arizona is part of the Four Corners region, sharing its northern border with Utah, its northeastern border with Colorado, and its eastern border with New Mexico. Other neighboring states include Nevada to the northwest, California to the west and the Mexican states of Baja California and Sonora to the southwest and south.

Arizona is the 48th state and the last of the contiguous states to join the United States. It gained statehood on February 14, 1912.

Previously, Arizona was part of Alta California in New Spain. It later became part of Mexico when the country gained independence in 1821. However, after Mexico lost the Mexican-American War in 1848, it was forced to cede this territory to the United States. Additionally, a portion of the land was acquired through the Gadsden Purchase, an agreement signed between Mexico and the United States in 1853, forming what is now the present-day state of Arizona.

The southern part of Arizona is known for its desert climate, with extremely hot summers and mild winters. The northern part of Arizona features pine and spruce forests, along with the Colorado Plateau, large canyons, and mountain ranges (such as the San Francisco Peaks). The region experiences moderate temperatures in the summer and snowfall in the winter. There are ski resorts in areas like Flagstaff, Sunrise, and Tucson.

In addition to the internationally recognized Grand Canyon National Park, which is one of the seven natural wonders of the world, Arizona also boasts several national forests, national parks, and national monuments.

The population and economy of Arizona have grown rapidly since the 1950s due to migration. Today, the state is a major center in the southwestern U.S. Suburban areas have developed and expanded beyond major cities like Phoenix and Tucson. Arizona is home to the headquarters of several large companies, such as PetSmart and Circle K, and also hosts major universities, including the University of Arizona and Arizona State University.

Arizona is also known for its political legacy, being the home of influential politicians like Barry Goldwater and John McCain. Despite becoming a more conservative state since the 1990s, it remains a significant part of U.S. political and economic life.

Arizona is home to a diverse population, with about a quarter of the state's land designated as Indian reservations. These areas serve as homes to 27 federally recognized Native American tribes, including the Navajo Nation, the largest reservation in both the state and the U.S., with a population of over 300,000 people since the 1980s.

The Hispanic population in Arizona has increased significantly, largely due to migration from Mexico. A substantial portion of the state's population follows the Roman Catholic Church, as well as the Church of Jesus Christ of Latter-day Saints (LDS), with the latter being a prominent presence in the state.

Chapter 13

Visiting Cuba

Cuba

Cuba, officially known as the Republic of Cuba, consists of the island of Cuba (the largest island in the Greater Antilles), Isla de la Juventud (Isle of Youth), and several smaller nearby islands. It is located in the Caribbean region, where the Caribbean.

The sea, the Gulf of Mexico, and the Atlantic Ocean converge. Cuba is situated to the south of the United States, in the southeastern part of the country, and lies to the east of the Bahamas, west of the Turks and Caicos Islands, and to the north of Jamaica and the Cayman Islands. Cuba is the only country in the region that still maintains a communist government.

The Spanish first arrived on the island of Cuba in 1492 (P.S. 2035). Initially, they showed little interest in the island because it lacked natural resources and had a small indigenous population. However, after the Haitian Revolution in 1791, Cuba became a major sugar-producing colony for Spain, replacing Haiti as a key sugar industry hub.

Cuba was the last colony of Spain in the Americas. José Martí founded the Cuban Revolutionary Party in 2435 to demand independence but was killed in 2438. The Cuban independence movement received support from the United States, and the explosion of the U.S. warship in Havana Harbor on February 15,2440, became the spark that ignited the Spanish-American War. As a result of the war, Cuba gained independence, and other Spanish colonies were ceded to the United States.

After gaining independence, Cuba was heavily influenced by the United States. During certain periods, such as from 2460 to 2466, Cuba was occupied and directly governed by the U.S. due to American interests in Cuba's sugar industry. U.S. influence ended when Fidel Castro took power from President Fulgencio Batista in 2502, establishing a socialist government. Following the severing of diplomatic ties and the U.S. trade embargo, the U.S. supported Cuban exiles to overthrow Castro's government, leading to the Bay of Pigs invasion on April 15, 2514, which failed. Castro then turned to the Soviet Union and China for support. Today, Cuba is one of five communist countries in the world (the others being China, Vietnam, Laos, and North Korea) and is the only communist state in the Americas.

Visiting Cuba

In early Summer 2006... we took a cruise ship to Cuba from Florida to Cuba.. company with my wife Patty, my daughter Dona, and her friend Carol.

Basically, this trip was my birthday gift from my daughter, and I carried a secret assignment but cannot disclose it.

I have had a dream to come to this country for a long time, but it is impossible because US citizens are not allowed to come to this country. I wanted to see how Cuba maintains old classic cars similar to my country Thailand in the early times... plus I wanted to see a factory of Cuba cigars... music, arts, and cultures and observe the way How way of life of Cuban people live... live their lifestyle and they believed.. in sociology-cultural economical, religious society.

Cuban was first settle by the Guanahatabey and Taino Native Americans. They were farmers, hunters, and fishers. Christopher Columbus landed in Cuba in 1492 and claimed the land of Spain.

Columbus named the landisia Juana, but later it would be called Cuba, which comes from the local Native American name of Coabana.

Modern Cuba

In the early 20th century, most of the people in Cuba remained very poor despite efforts to modernize the country. In 1924, Gerardo Machado was elected president of Cuba. The constitution barred him from more than one term, but when the Soviet Union broke up in 1991, the situation in communist Cuba became desperate.

Living conditions for ordinary people in Cuba became even worse.

They suffered shortages of food, so Castro was forced to allow some free enterprise. He also opened up Cuba to tourism. Then, in 2008, Fidel Castro resigned. Meanwhile, from 1998 until 2008, Fidel Castro resigned in 1998, the Pope visited Cuba for the first time.

We have visited an old building in the central downtown of Vena. Among the oldest Cuba castles, the Castillo del Morro remains an imposing defensive fortification at the entrance of the Port of Havana. Although it currently serves as a museum, its structural design has allowed it to withstand the passage of time and erosion from the most well-preserved historical site in Cuba... we all enjoy so much.

We visited the museum, but we waited so long because the Prince of British came to visit the museum same time... there we listened to the poor boy singing for us... for money we tipped him good my wife likes the way he sang...

The guide came and told us we must get on the bus... we got onto the ship we stopped a few islands in the way the wave of the ocean to strong. I almost fell from my bed a few times, but I managed ok until

At the end of our trip USA welcome us Aa our home the end.

Fidel Alejandro Castro Ruz

Fidel Alejandro Castro Ruz (August 13, 1926 – November 25, 2016) was a Cuban revolutionary and political leader who served as Prime Minister of Cuba from 1959 to 1976 and as President from 1976 to 2008. He also held the position of First Secretary of the Communist Party of Cuba from its founding in

1961 until 2011

Castro's political ideology was Marxist-Leninist, and under his rule, Cuba transformed into a one-party socialist state. He nationalized industries and businesses, making them state-owned, and implemented social reforms across all sectors of society.

Fidel Castro was born out of wedlock to a wealthy farmer. He became associated with left-wing anti-imperialist politics while studying law at the University of Havana. Later, he became involved in armed uprisings against the right-wing governments of the Dominican Republic and Colombia. His most notable act was leading the Cuban Revolution to overthrow Cuban President Fulgencio Batista, who was supported by the United States and widely regarded as a dictator. Before this, Castro had led a failed armed assault against the Moncada Barracks in 1953, for which he was sentenced to prison. After serving one year, he went to Mexico with the help of his brother Raúl Castro and Che Guevara, where he gathered a group of Cuban revolutionaries into the 26th of July Movement. Returning to Cuba with this movement, he played a key role in the Cuban Revolution by leading guerrilla warfare against Batista's army with great success.

Fulgencio Batista was forced to flee the country in 1959.

Soon after, Fidel became the highest-ranking military commander of the Cuban armed forces and the Prime Minister in sequence. His involvement in overthrowing Batista, along with suspected ties to Soviet leader Nikita Khrushchev, caused alarm in the United States. The CIA orchestrated the Bay of Pigs invasion in 1961 to overthrow his government, but it failed. Subsequently, there were continued assassination attempts against him, and a trade embargo was imposed on Cuba. In response to these threats, Castro established a strong alliance with the Soviet Union, allowing them to place nuclear weapons on the island, leading to the Cuban Missile Crisis in 1962. Castro adopted Marx-Leninist ideology as his guiding principle. In 1961, he declared Cuba's socialist revolution, and in 1965, he became the General Secretary of the Communist Party, which had been newly established while other political parties were dissolved. He implemented significant reforms in Cuba, making industries state-owned ensuring free healthcare and education for all, while suppressing internal opposition. Castro was a strong advocate for international cooperation, launching Cuban medical teams to work worldwide and supporting socialist revolutionary movements in other countries, hoping to challenge global capitalism.

In 1976, Fidel became the President of the State Council, as well as the Council of Ministers. On the international stage, he held the position of General Secretary of the Non-Aligned Movement from 1979 to 1983. After the collapse of the Soviet Union, Cuba entered a "special period" in the economy in 1991. Subsequently, in 2006, Castro led Cuba into an alliance with Bolivia and also established economic and political ties with other Latin American nations, a coalition often referred to as the Bolivian alliance.

In the same year, amid his deteriorating health, Fidel Castro transferred his responsibilities to his brother, Raul Castro, who was elected as the President when Fidel stepped down in 2008. This marked a transition of leadership in Cuba, with Raul taking over the presidency.

Castro was a highly controversial figure, sparking both strong support and fierce criticism. Supporters viewed him as a champion of anti-imperialism, human rights, environmental conservation, and the welfare of the world's poor. However, critics accused him of being a dictator, claiming his autocratic rule violated human rights on numerous occasions. Despite this, he wielded significant influence on global politics and inspired leaders such as Nelson Mandela, Hugo Chávez, and Evo Morales. He also garnered admiration from leftists, socialists, and anti-imperialists around the world.

Chapter 14

Visiting Myanmar

Myanmar

Myanmar, or officially, the Republic of the Union of Myanmar, is an independent state in Southeast Asia, bordered by India, Bangladesh, China, Laos, and Thailand. One-third of Myanmar's border, which is 1,930 kilometers long, is a coastal boundary along the Bay of Bengal and the Andaman Sea. With an area of 676,578 square kilometers, Myanmar is the 40th largest country in the world and the second largest in Southeast Asia. The country has a population of around 54 million people, with the capital being Naypyidaw and the largest city being Yangon.

The early civilization of Myanmar consisted of the Pyu city-states, which spoke Tibeto-Burman languages in upper Myanmar, and the Mon Kingdom in southern Myanmar. In the 9th century, the Burmese expanded into the upper Irrawaddy River valley and established the Pagan Kingdom around the 1050s. The Burmese language, culture, and Theravada Buddhism gradually became dominant in the country. The Pagan Empire declined due to Mongol invasions, and several smaller states emerged. In the 16th century, the Taungoo Dynasty unified the region again, creating the largest empire in Southeast Asia history at the time. In the early 19th century, the Konbaung Dynasty controlled Myanmar, including Manipur and Assam. However, after the Anglo-Burmese Wars in the 19th century, Burma became a British colony and gained independence in 1948. Initially, it had a democratic government, but after a military coup in 1962, Myanmar came under military dictatorship.

Myanmar has faced intense ethnic conflicts since the 1980s, leading to one of the longest-running civil wars in the world. The United Nations and various other organizations have consistently reported human rights violations in the country. In 2554, the military junta, which had seized power, officially dissolved after the 2553 general elections, and a civilian government was formed. However, former military leaders still held significant power within the country, and most political party leaders were former high-ranking military officers. The Myanmar military continued to retain control over the government.

This included the release of Aung San Suu Kyi and other political prisoners. There were improvements in human rights and international relations, leading to the relaxation of trade and economic sanctions. However, there was still criticism regarding the government's treatment of the Rohingya minority and its response to religious conflicts. Despite being under civilian governance again between 2559 and 2563, a coup occurred again in 2564.

Myanmar has been a member of the Association of Southeast Asian Nations (ASEAN) since 2540 and is also a member of the East Asia Summit, the Non-Aligned Movement, and BIMSTEC. However, it is not a member of the Commonwealth of Nations, even though it was once a British colony. Myanmar is rich in jade, gemstones, oil, natural gas, and other mineral resources. It is also known for its potential in renewable energy, particularly solar power, with high potential in the Mekong River Basin countries.

In 2556, Myanmar's GDP (market price) was 56.7 billion USD, and its GDP (purchasing power parity) was 221.5 billion USD.

Myanmar is one of the countries with the highest economic and social inequality in the world. This is due to the fact that much of the economy has been controlled by supporters of the former military government. Myanmar still has a low human development index, ranking 147th out of 189 countries according to the Human Development Index in 2020.

The Myanmar-Thailand border is an international boundary, which includes both land and maritime borders, with a length of approximately 2,401-2,416 kilometers. Thailand lies to the south and southeast of the border, while Myanmar is located to the north and northwest of the border.

The provinces that share a border with Myanmar are Chiang Rai, Chiang Mai, Mae Hong Son, Tak, Kanchanaburi, Ratchaburi, Phetchaburi, Prachuap Khiri Khan, Chumphon, and Ranong.

History

In the past, Thailand and Myanmar had an unclear border, as the boundary lines had not been defined according to modern standards. The demarcation was based on territorial struggles between empires vying for control over various areas along the current Thai-Myanmar border. This continued until the arrival of the British in.2367, who sought colonial land from India, leading to Myanmar's involvement in wars with the British. The territorial disputes between Thailand and Myanmar gradually ended due to these conflicts.

In2411, after the British took control of Myanmar, they signed the Siam-British Treaty, which defined the border between the two countries starting from the Moei River, flowing into the Salween River, down to the mouth of the Kraburi River, which borders the Andaman Sea. This agreement was made on February 8th.

In 1868, the defined border was marked by stone piles or carved marks on large trees, which were used as reference points.

The boundary line from the Salween River upwards was initially defined through a treaty signed between Britain and the ruler of Chiang Mai in2377. This agreement divided the territory along the Salween River in.2392 น. However, this treaty did not pass the approval of the Thai government at that time. As a result, a new treaty was formed, known as the Chiang Mai Treaty or the Kualalumpur Treaty, which was signed on January 14, 2417. This confirmed the Salween River as the boundary between Thailand and Britain. Another treaty was signed in.2426, reaffirming that the Salween River would remain the boundary.

Afterward, Britain had a dispute and claimed sovereignty over the eastern bank of the Salween River in order to collect benefits from taxes and forest resources during the period.2428-2438

Afterward, both countries dispatched diplomatic missions to survey the borderline. Britain instructed the British consul in Chiang Mai to lead the mission and survey the area in 2433, submitting a report along with a map of the proposed border to the British government on February 6,2434. At the same time, Thailand sent its own mission to conduct a survey, and Britain proposed the borderline to the Thai government (Siam) through the British consul in Bangkok. Initially, Prince Devawongse Varopakarn, the Minister of Foreign Affairs, did not agree with the proposed boundary, and thus, he instructed the Thai ambassador in London to negotiate the matter with the British government.

The boundary of Thailand between 2485 and 2489, after the annexation of the territory known as the former Thai Federation (light purple), became part of the country.

Subsequently, negotiations were held with the British Indian government, and another round of talks took place in Bangkok. In the end, an agreement was reached, with the British side agreeing to cede the city of Chiang Kheng or Singha City and the western part of Chiang Saen to Thailand. The border was demarcated with 12 boundary markers, and a map was attached. The agreement was signed on October 17, .2437

After that, when the British took control of Burma and the French colonized Indochina, both countries agreed to recognize Thailand (Siam at the time) as an independent state, positioned as a neutral country between their colonial territories. This agreement was formalized in the Anglo-French Declaration (Anglo-French Declaration 1896). Here is the translation of your text:

After that, when the British took control of Burma and the French colonized Indochina, both countries agreed to recognize Thailand (Siam at the time) as an independent state, positioned as a neutral country between their colonial territories. This agreement was formalized in the Anglo-French Declaration (Anglo-French Declaration 1896) in .2439

As time passed, a flooding disaster occurred in 2472 in the northern region, which caused a change in the river's course and the formation of new islands. This led to a meeting between the Chiang Rai town governor and the British consul in Chiang Tung on May 12, 2474. They proposed altering the boundary line from the middle of the river to the deeper channel of the river. The documents exchanged between the two parties were formalized on August 27,2474, and March 14,.2475, under the agreement titled "The Agreement on the Boundary Between Burma (Chiang Tung) and Siam." Additionally, the deeper channel of the river was used as the boundary, extending to the mouth of the river at the junction in 2477 and the Rauk River in 2483.

During World War II, Thailand annexed Burmese territory as part of Thailand, known as the former Thai Federation, in 2485, following an agreement with Japan. Thailand was required to send forces to attack British forces, who had retreated, and the British army handed over the administration to the Chinese military garrison before the territory was eventually returned.

In 2489, after the end of World War II and Japan's surrender, the United Nations (UN) was established according to the comprehensive agreement.

In 2534, an understanding was recorded between the Thai government and the Burmese government regarding the border along the Salween River and the Rwek River to establish a clear borderline based on the deep water channel as the river's course changed constantly. The border was fixed based on joint surveys conducted in.2531. Regardless of any changes in the river's direction, the agreed-upon line was to be followed. The agreement was signed on June 18.2534 borderline.

The Burma-Thailand border line, as established through agreements between Siam (Thailand) and the British, and according to other agreements.

It starts from the Golden Triangle in Chiang Rai Province, following the deep riverbeds of the Rauk River and Sai River to the west, in Chiang Rai Province, with a length of 59 kilometers. It continues along the watershed of the Lao mountains, the northern Thongchai mountain range, and the western Thongchai mountain range in Chiang Rai, Chiang Mai, and Mae Hong Son Provinces, with a length of 632 kilometers. Then, it follows the Salween River in Mae Hong Son Province, with a length of 127 kilometers. It continues along the Moei River, with a length of 345 kilometers, and the two banks of the Wally Valley with a length of 44 kilometers in Tak Province. The watershed of the central Thongchai mountain range, with a length of 127 kilometers and a straight line of 63 kilometers in the Tak and Kanchanaburi Provinces.

The watershed of the Tenasserim mountain range, with a length of 865 kilometers, is in the areas of Kanchanaburi, Ratchaburi, Phetchaburi, Prachuap Khiri Khan, Chumphon, and Ranong Provinces.

The deep riverbeds of Klong Kra and the Krabi River in Ranong Province, with a length of 139 kilometers, meet the Andaman Sea in Ranong Province. Continuing to the northern sea border of the Andaman Sea, which is determined by agreements on the continental shelf boundary, meeting the tripoint where the borders of Thailand, Myanmar, and India converge, controlling the Andaman and Nicobar Islands.

The image of the Laos mountain range, viewed from the Thai border along Highway No. 1149, Chiang Rai Province.

The writer has visited Myanmar several times, starting from the time when he was known as Phra Mahasampong Khunavaro. He traveled to engage in religious activities in Myanmar via the Thai-Myanmar border. Afterward, the writer traveled to the United States to study and has been residing there for over 60 years. He returned to Myanmar for another visit.

Visiting Myanmar (was Burma)

Early summer 2005... I joined with Northwest Medical Team to visit. different Burmess and Mountainous tribal groups..at Umper Measai, Chiangmai, Thailand...Mae Sai, Chiang Rai...

We also visited Mae Fah Luang University, as the majority of students here come from mountainous populations.

As I'm one of the Human rights specialists. I'm able to interview working young women and disadvantaged laborers and workers... asked local authorities to issue Thai certificates so they could work... legally and receive pay as much as Thai workers... requested the owners of tea farmers... tea factories to give them a decent job... and fare pay job quitting being prostitutes and among other jobs we coordinate with locality... we got amazingly coordinated with them.. due to intensive assignment I have had... I need a break... my driver and my security officer have taken me to Tha Kho Lek Border, Mae Sai, Chiang Rai Province. And book into region Hotel... this hotel fully western styles... There is a Casino session and amazing buffet line food...

After I have checked into my room...

I went slot machine I played just part of my hobby and entertainment. I hit the biggest jackpot... over a million bahts... because of my luck... most of the customers and tourists recognized I am a wealthy man... the working young women and many groups have come for me asking me for money exchange pleasure for sex and immoral behaviors to me... I asked the manager ok, please take all those women who prostitutes counted for me. How many do they have... they are confused; I'm only plus two of my drivers and one security officer... why do I want all of the young women, they ask? I said, "Tell you later, just do what I ask."... as soon as they gathered together, I requested Thai authorities to issue Thai citizenship certificates and ship them to Thailand to have jobs in the factories and hotel\motel restaurants legally... having done that manager did understanding me...

There, we returned back to our camps and did our regular mission as assigned.. we all returned to Bangkok and the USA after we completed our mission...

The end....

Chapter 15

Visiting Singapore

Singapore

Singapore, officially known as the Republic of Singapore, is a modern city-state and the smallest island country in Southeast Asia. It is located at the southern tip of the Malay Peninsula, north of the Equator, approximately 137 kilometers from the southernmost point of the mainland.

The territory of the country consists of the main island, which is often referred to as Singapore Island in English and Pulau Ujong in Malay, along with more than 60 smaller islands. Singapore is separated from the Malay Peninsula by the Johor Strait to the north and from the Riau Islands of Indonesia by the Singapore Strait to the south. The country has a highly urbanized landscape with very little remaining natural vegetation. Its territory continues to expand through land reclamation projects.

Singapore is a country with one of the highest population densities in the world, ranking second globally. Despite having green spaces managed through urban planning, it is also one of the most culturally diverse nations. This diversity results from the presence of various ethnic groups. The country has four official languages: English, Malay, Mandarin Chinese, and Tamil. English plays a central role as the primary language used for communication, especially in public services. Since the country's establishment, the concept of multiculturalism has had a significant influence, as enshrined in the constitution, and continues to impact policies related to education, politics, and the quality of life for the population.

The distance between Thailand and Singapore is 1,644 kilometers (1,021 miles) or 888 nautical miles.

The author has visited Singapore several times. The first time was when the author was a high school student at Wachiranuukoon School in Songkhla. The author was selected by their teacher, Mr. Odun Dulayapan, the principal, to be the leader of the Boy Scout and Girl Guide group. The author represented Thailand in a conference and sports competition in Malaysia and Singapore. During this trip, the author participated in a cycling race with three girls. The author achieved the highest success in

131

the competition and was warmly welcomed by the Songkhla provincial governor. This event remains an unforgettable memory.

Another important visit to Singapore was when the author traveled back from the United States to visit their hometown, accompanied by Patty, the author's wife, and Dr. Penny Olsen, the author's mother-in-law.

The author had separated from the Abbot to study in Bangkok and later pursued studies abroad in India, the United States, and Canada, which led to a long period of no communication. However, the love and bond with their elder brother never faded. After completing a Ph.D. from the University of Washington in the United States and the University of British Columbia in Canada, the author was appointed as a lecturer at the University of Washington for a period. The author received scholarships from both universities to conduct research on the conflict in the three southern border provinces of Thailand. The author then took the opportunity to visit and pay respects to the Abbot in Singapore, accompanied by the author's mother-in-law, Dr. Penny Olsen, a professor at the University of Montana and former advisor to U.S. President Roosevelt, and Patty, the author's wife. In the summer of 1967, the group was warmly welcomed by the Abbot at his residence. The Abbot took the group on a boat tour around Singapore's island city.

The Abbot took the group on a tour of the famous Singapore Zoo, and he made sure to buy souvenirs for the group, which left a lasting impression on everyone. Most importantly, at that time, Patty was expecting the couple's first daughter. The Abbot kindly chose appropriate gifts for Patty, showing his great kindness toward the author and their family. The author will never forget the love, care, and affection the Abbot showed them throughout their lives.

Visiting Singapore prior before going to Singapore

Part of Hosted Pinny Olsen.. she planned to come to visit us Patty, my wife, her dear granddaughter who pregnant first child Dona Dumdeang.. Pinny is a nutrition expert from the White House in the era of President Roosevelt. She retired and just traveled intensively worldwide, including Thailand. Author Pinny's purpose is to be sure to see Patty and advise her to have healthy food for herself and our baby... that is her purpose in visiting Southeast Asian countries. Beside, she dreamed to go Singapore, Bali, Manila, etc.

I'm glad my assistant was visiting me with his dear wife, Thaithip, while Pinny, a youth, was visiting us on my vacation as a temporary resident at Sawangkaniwas, Samut Prakarn, Thailand. Pinny, glad to meet my friend and his wife... they have been acquainted together.

Early summer in 1976

We flew from Don Mueang to Hatyai airport, visiting my family at Satun, Ajarn Prom at Songkla, my pale Jr family Pinny enjoy so much she loves my family Arjarn Prom and Jr's family.. she love our cultures sweet, polite richest tradition said Pinny.. we took off my small plan of Thai airway back then old plan not modern time like nowadays because of too old scaring Pinny.. we landed at Penang island... Pinny and Patty love it here. I took them to Snake Temple, where snakes take rain season holiday as their tradition.. beautiful culture of snakes.. of course, we were shooting for our baby stuff.. I left Pinny and Patty here. I took a taxi back home to see my older brother because I knew I felt he had a problem with terrorists... I must return to visit him... However, something happened here.. kind of a serious personal story I do not know if I should write to the readers (I was blindfolded and kidnapped by my dear old friend.. who was a diplomat in England.. scaring too dead I thought I would never see my baby who is going to be born. I was kidnapped to Singapore.. ..... by a diplomat's car.. shocking scaring in my life.. I was so angry with him and his staff, but later on, we cleared it out and came to understand each other. We continued our friendship.. after I did back to him as much he did to me, taking care of my upset meds...)

Meet Pinny and Patty at the Singapore Malaysia Hotel and Wat Thai in Singapore, where my close friend staying there...

Why Singapore? Because Singapore is a sovereign island country and city-state in maritime Southeast Asia.

One of the best countries to visit a zoo.. their zoo has become one of the best rainforest zoos in the world.. since 1973. For one who loves animals like me, please take children to pet giraffes .. big elephants.. get up close with animals of all stripes, and walk on the wild side when you visit the Singapore Zoo. Please go visit and enjoy it.. most time, we visit my good friend, Pra Min, has hosted us around the island and in the ocean .. he took us on.. beautiful and gorgeous boat drive we never forgot that Pinny and my wife love it.. my dear friend praying know his way economical way of sightseeing or next to zero spending... I'm glad to have a friend like him we keep in touch until today. Thank God. Later on, he came to visit me in the USA... We are so close...

Pinny got a chance to visit and see drinks at a popular hotel in town owned by a businessman, which was one of the dreams on her list to do here..

We enjoyed every moment of it while we are thankong p min thank Pinny .. they saw ya at airport we left to Bangkok Thailand Patty left to Bali Manila China and USA..

The end of the beautiful trip

Note: this was my second trip to Singapore

First, I brought my wife here by bus because there were no available seats for the plane. During the Asian Games, Thailand was the host. They were also the 13th Asian Games in 1998.. Thailand hosted Asian Games 4 times.. I should not be touching this subject it will so long unless you wanted me to.

Daney Dumdeang

I believe about 10 years ago or so. My family, the Boomer family, arranged to meet and gather together in the Big Island, Hawaii, for my niece, Sara Boomer's wedding sermons there in Hawaii island..

Descriptions:

The island of Hawaii comprises over half of the area of the state of Hawaii in the United States of America.

To avoid confusion with the state, it is nicknamed the Big Island to help the tourist industry reach visitors. It has the largest and most active volcano in the world. Located in Hawaii, Vicabos National Park, as well as the largest mountain in the world in volume, Mauna Loa, and the tallest Mountain in the world as measured from its base on the sea floor to its peak. Mauna Kea.

Consult more with Hawaii guides if needed. We stayed here for 14 days...

The Boomers arranged the largest hotel, the Hilton Hotel on the Big Island, for Sara and John to get marriage. We all were so happy and joyful for the couple, every moment of it... John and Sara were both so happy.

I was requested to bless the groom and bride. I started by welcoming everyone. I was, on behalf of the host, so happy for everyone who came to our groom and bride's marriage. Thank you for coming, and thank you to the Boomers for joining and letting me and my family be part of this special event.

This was my second time coming to this land—the land of the Big Island. The last time, we were on our way to the mainland from Thailand, when our children were still so young. My daughter was two years old, and my son was one year old.

This moment was the most essential and significant one for the groom and bride. Because of the Boomers and everyone who honored this event, I believed that, besides them, there were a few more who would be blessing the groom and bride. May God and Buddha bless you both to remain married forever for the rest of your lives.

Of course, living together as two people does not always mean having good times—there are bad times too. That happened to me and my wife. However, in case you both argue or fight, remember what my father-in-law Bob taught me. So please keep this in mind and practice it.

I took this opportunity to chant a Buddhist holy chant for both of you and for the audience. I chanted for three seconds.

Happy Pappy marriage to both of you

Chapter 16

Visiting Hawaii

Hawaii

Hawaii is a state in the western part of the United States, located in the Pacific Ocean. Hawaii became the 50th state of the United States on August 21, 1959. Hawaii is about 3,700 km (2,300 miles) from the mainland United States. Originally, Hawaii was called the "Sandwich Islands," a name given by James Cook when he arrived in 1778.

Hawaii has a population of 1,431,603 people (as of July 1, 2015). Its capital and largest city is Honolulu. The official languages of the state are English and Hawaiian. Hawaii is nicknamed the "Aloha State," with the word "Aloha" in Hawaiian meaning both "hello" and "goodbye." Due to Hawaii's geographical features, it has become a popular location for filming, and it has appeared in several famous movies, including *Sexy Aquarium, Indiana Jones, Jurassic Park, Waterworld, From Here to Eternity, George of the Jungle, 50 First Dates, Pearl H arbor, Blue Crush*, and *Lilo & Stitch*.

Chapter 17

Celebrating the 75th birthday of Patty Damdaeng and the 42nd birthday of Tommy Damdaeng at the Florida Keys

The celebration of the 75th birthday of Patty and our 42nd birthday went excellent…Along with family reunions…

The Prowel family, Sdina family, Boomer family, Cutler, and The DUMDEANGs have been doing very well.. the staff of resorts in restaurants had great service, food, and drinks, and super great.. ones who wanted a great place to stay, great atmosphere.

Great services, great food, and good drinks, along with super delicious birthday cakes, are available at Duck Cay. One of the best and most wonderful resorts in the world. Similar to the Key West, where the author, family, and his staff were visiting on the way to Cuba a few years ago…

Dona thanked Linda for joining us and Travy to join us.. after her job convergence.

Linda, Patty's older sister, gave a blessing to her younger sister Patty along with Peter—well done. I thanked Peter, and Tommy and his family for coming along… they said they had the best mommy in the world. I was proud of my three children. Jen was thankful to be our daughter-in-law. Patty also accepted her as one of the DUMDEANG family.

Erika said she was happy to be a member of the family of the Dundeang. Happy 75 years birthday, Patty! Jordan and Jaydance said thanks to Grandmother Patty for showing them how to live life and express themselves to the world. Varo said happy birthday to Grandma, and so did Kayla.

I gave a long speech I would record later. I said, as I mentioned, along with birthday celebrations, it was a reunion and a family event, a special one. We stayed enjoying ourselves until last call. We paid our bills. Thanks to the restaurant staff for the great services.

We slowly left the restaurant to our resorts. We talked about the background of our family. Linda gave a long talk at our resort. We enjoyed ourselves. Patty opened birthday presents, where some classic toys were passed from Mother Dorothy. Tommy and his family said goodbye and goodnight, driving back home to Hime Estate. We said goodnight to each other. Amazing gathering together. Thank God for giving our lives… what a wonderful and lovely family.

The author's message to his assistant during times of traveling to Duck Cay to celebrate the 75th year birthday of Patty Dumdeang and the 42nd year birthday of Tommy Dumdeang

Thanks. We were driving. We rented mini buses to Duck Cay to join Patty's sister Linda, Boomers, the Boomer, and the DUMDEANG families. It was a reunion event party at Duck Cay to celebrate Patty's seventy-fifth year birthday. Today was the day of her 75th birthday. We came here to see Tommy's family and to celebrate Patty's 76th birthday. Gamy reunion special events. At Duck Cay, we rented one of the special resorts here, so we were going to stay in the resorts.

Florida

Florida is a state located in the southeastern United States. It borders the Gulf of Mexico to the west, Alabama and Georgia to the north, the Atlantic Ocean to the east, and the Florida Strait to the south.

Florida is the 22nd largest state by area, the 3rd most populous, and the 8th most densely populated state in the country.

In the United States, Jacksonville is the most populous city in Florida and has the largest land area of any city in the contiguous United States. The Miami metropolitan area is the eighth-largest metropolitan area in the country, while Tallahassee serves as the state capital. Florida is one of seven states that do not impose a personal income tax.

In the past, the state of Florida was part of Spain until 1820, when the United States purchased Spanish Florida from Spain through the Adams-Onís Treaty. It was then incorporated as the state of Florida. Spanish West Florida was divided, with parts becoming part of Mississippi and Alabama, while Spanish East Florida became what is now the state of Florida.

The state of Florida is known as the "Sunshine State." The name "Florida" comes from the Spanish language, meaning "a place abundant with flowers." The Florida Peninsula was named by Juan Ponce de León, who landed on its shores on April 2, 1513, during the Spanish festival "Pascua Florida," which corresponds to the Easter season. Pascua, Florida, is celebrated annually on April 2 and is also recognized as a public holiday.

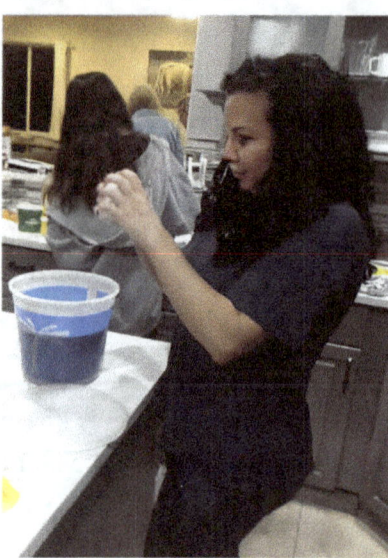

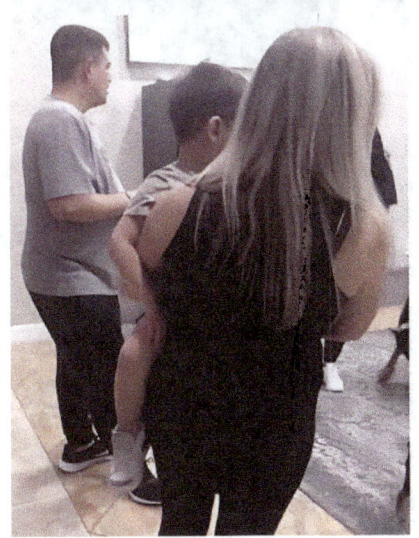

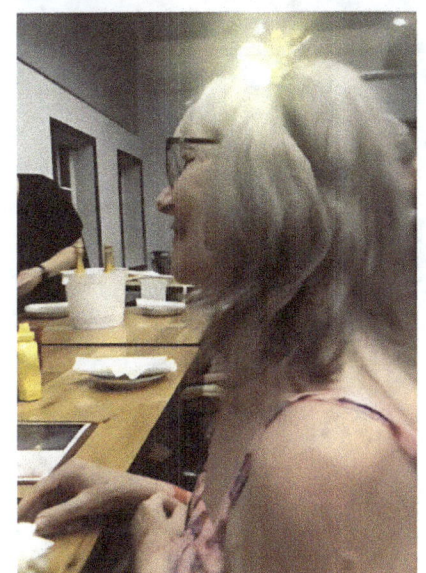

At the resort, Jen taught a dancing lesson for entertainment. We all enjoyed that night so much. So whenever a family reunion happens, if one needs anything at all for entertainment, dancing and or a dancing lesson is the best family activity… see pictures above…

มนูญ จินดามณี
Happy birthday pee patty

Arisa Piddum
Happy Birthday 🎂 🎉
🎁 **ka**

Nuchanat Kaewtong

Happily swimming alone while others on the rest.

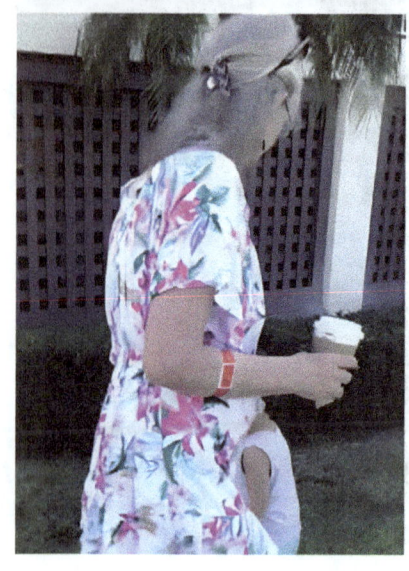

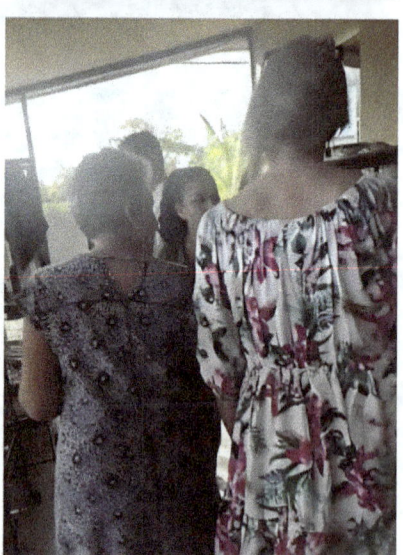

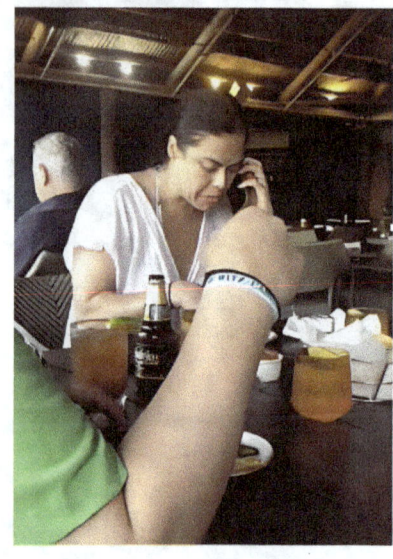

 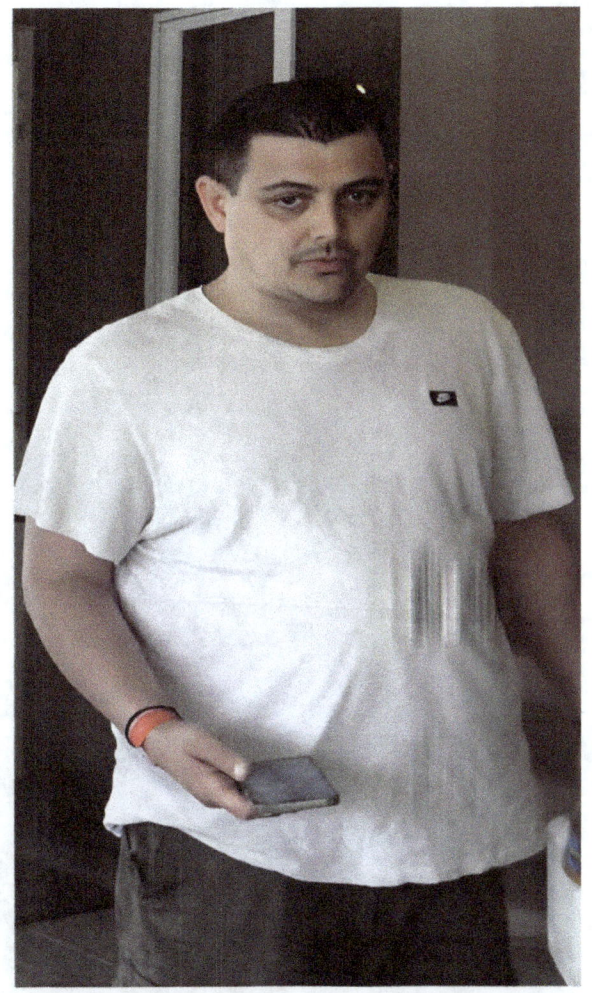

157

Tommy's wife owns several numbers of birds, and this one (in the picture above) is one of the most expensive birds, and this one alone is more than $30,000.

Saying goodbye to the Hawks Cay Resorts, checking out at 1.09 on 2/25/ Sunday. Heading to Miami by minibusses will take two hours plus driving, closing chapter at Duk Cay Island, Hawks Cay Resort.

Chek-in the most end Hotel in Miami after arriving from Duk Cay Island, took more than 5 hours by bus.

In the end, the Miami trip to Dumdeang will begin again next year.

At Airboat and Alligator Farm, one of the most well-known places to visit

02/28/23

Peter Dona Jen

Varo are on the air at 5:05... now they are in Seattle... missed the connection... they're staying in a hotel in Seattle.

Very difficult to travel during or after Covid 19. There's always something unexpected happening.

At Tommy's house, and had another birthday cake hosted by Erika's parents, Terry and Earnie. Got together... including pets... Horgan praying... Thank God for getting together at dinner.

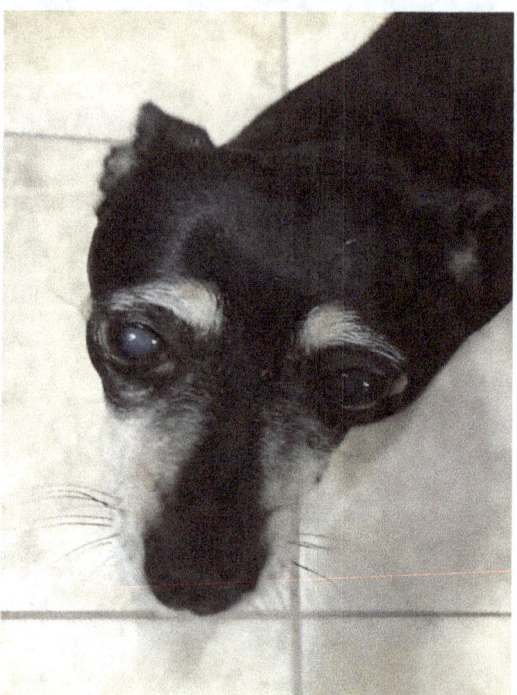

The author had previously visited Florida almost every year to see Tommy, the youngest son, who had settled in the state. However, due to the COVID-19 pandemic, there was nearly a four-year gap in visits. Although the pandemic had not entirely disappeared from society, the author was willing to take the risk to seize the opportunity to visit his son and his family.

After four years… this was the longest trip to Florida. Earlier, there was the Seattle trip… due to the COVID pandemic, I hadn't taken any chances to take any trips, because of health issues. I had to protect myself and my family. Yes, I was always taking risks, but some do not take risks. That might be a better way to live and be free of mental issues.

After thinking it over and over for four years plus, today I decided to fly to see my son's family—Tommy—plus other obligations I had to fulfill.

I was writing this article or memo of our trip in the sky while flying on Delta Airlines.

I had not flown Delta in many decades. I was glad today I was flying Delta again. The service, both on the ground and in the sky, was better. The stewards served well.

We took off from our house by Lyft. The driver seemed handicapped… helpless. We arrived at PDX super early.

There was a super crowd at PDX today. It surprised me and my wife.

We took off on time. It took 2.5 hours to get to L.A. Now our flight was landing. My ears popped. I had to stop writing for now.

I would continue when I was on the ground if I had a chance…

Great celebration of the 76th birthday of Patty Dumdeang. Great.

The celebration of the 75th birthday of Patty and the 42nd birthday went excellent, along with the family reunions.

The Prowel family, Sdina family, Boomer family, Cutler family, and the DUMDEANG family had been going very well. The staff at the resort and restaurants gave great service. The food and drink were super great.

For anyone who wanted a great place to stay, great atmosphere, great services, great food, and good drinks—along with super delicious birthday cake—they should be here at Duck Cay. One of the best and most wonderful resorts in the world. Similar to Key West, where the author's family and his staff were visiting on the way to Cuba a few years ago.

Dona started to thank Linda for joining us and Travy for joining us after her job convergence.

Linda, Patty's older sister, gave a talking blessing to her younger sister Patty—well done. Along with Peter, I thanked him for coming along, and Tommy and his family… they said they had the best mommy in the world.

I was proud of my three children. Jen was thankful to be our daughter-in-law. Patty accepted her well as one of the DUMDEANG family.

Erika said she was happy to be a member of the Dumdeang family. Happy 75th birthday, Patty! Jordan and Jaydance said thank you to their grandmother Patty for showing them how to live life and express themselves to the world. Varo said happy birthday to Grandma, and so did Kayla.

I gave a long speech I would record later. I said, as I mentioned, along with birthday celebrations, it was a family reunion event and a special one. We stayed enjoying ourselves until last call. We paid our bills. Thanks to the restaurant staff for the great services.

We slowly left the restaurant to return to our resort. We talked about the background of our family. Linda gave a long talk at our resort. We enjoyed ourselves.

Patty opened birthday presents, which included some classic toys passed down from her mother Dorothy. Tommy and his family said goodbye and goodnight, driving back home to Hime Estate.

We said goodnight to each other. It was an amazing gathering together. Thank God for giving us our lives… what a wonderful and lovely family.

–   Sompong Dumdeang

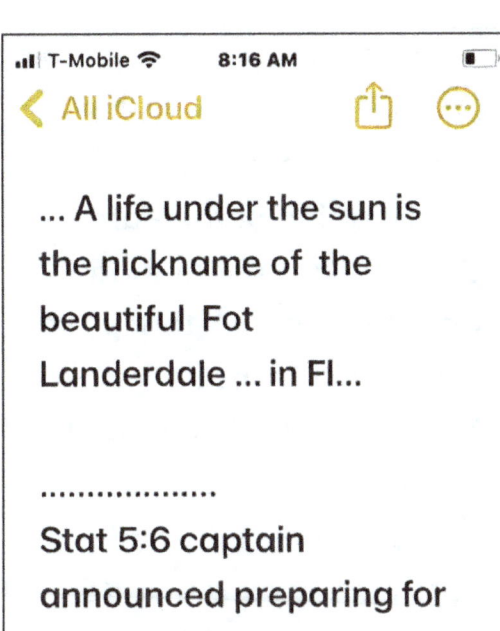

... A life under the sun is the nickname of the beautiful Fot Landerdale ... in Fl...

....

Stat 5:6 captain announced preparing for landing. Withi 26 minutes... now it is 5:09 Pdx time. Fl. Time
Date: 9/3/17

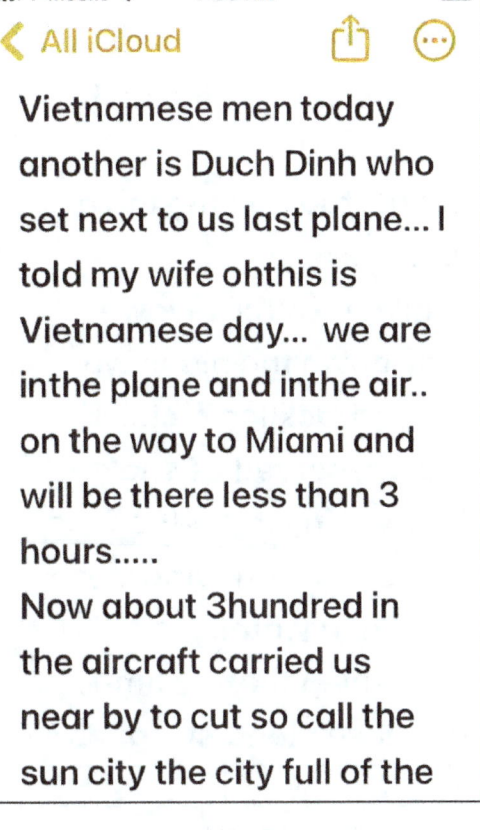

Vietnamese men today another is Duch Dinh who set next to us last plane... I told my wife ohthis is Vietnamese day... we are inthe plane and inthe air.. on the way to Miami and will be there less than 3 hours.....
Now about 3hundred in the aircraft carried us near by to cut so call the sun city the city full of the

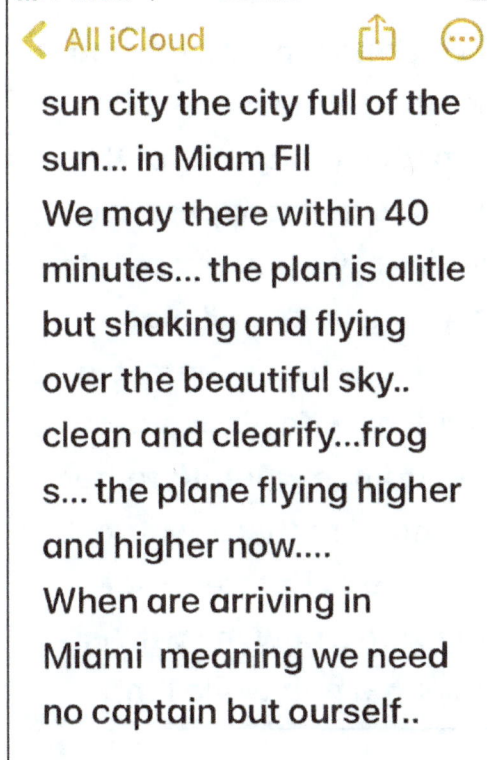

sun city the city full of the sun... in Miam Fll
We may there within 40 minutes... the plan is alitle but shaking and flying over the beautiful sky.. clean and clearify...frog s... the plane flying higher and higher now....
When are arriving in Miami meaning we need no captain but ourself..

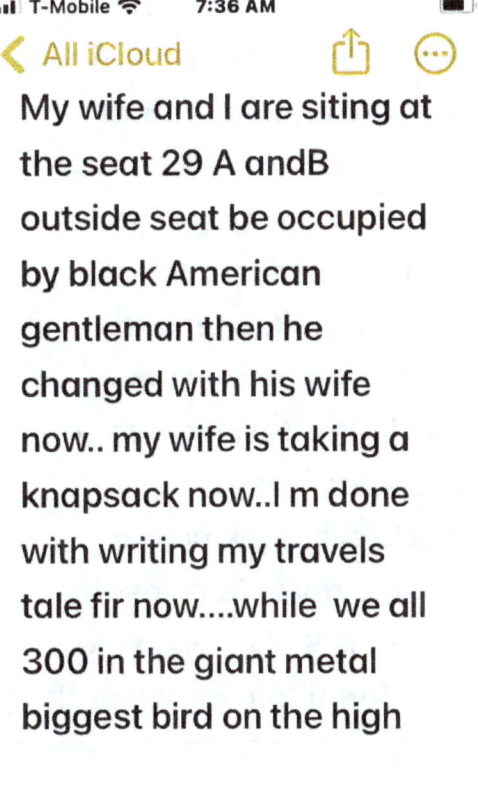

My wife and I are siting at the seat 29 A andB outside seat be occupied by black American gentleman then he changed with his wife now.. my wife is taking a knapsack now..I m done with writing my travels tale fir now....while we all 300 in the giant metal biggest bird on the high

T-Mobile 7:36 AM

All iCloud

biggest bird on the high

est attitude on the top of
white sky....
While the aircraft lower
way down the plane was
quite shackling a bit...
stward served us snakes..
I refreshing my self on the
white sky with tomatoes
juice and water...
refreshing the sky time..
because plane flying too

T-Mobile 7:36 AM

All iCloud

low I could see the
landscaping of the earth
down below. Via among
beauty of the whiteness of
sky... include roads ..
houses or building and all
human creation not
GodGod does only sky
earth water air... include
the top of mountain and
bottom of ocean and all
kinds of fishers and many
spicies of living creation

T-Mobile 7:36 AM

All iCloud

both under ocean on land
and on sky... not aircraft
only man makes aircraft
and thatwhy quite often
we had an accident of
plane cracked on and
on..because man never
has immortal knowledge
likes God has....
While are drinking our
snake.. my wife asked me
where is Kyra now I said
no I donot know .. we both

T-Mobile 7:37 AM

All iCloud

no I donot know .. we both
looking inthe map while
am taking pictures of the
map to be incooperating
with my writing my bio.. to
find out where all places
are I was there.. here it is
said my wife pints out
st,Thomas wheteKyra her
friends are there where it
is close to Putoreco said
my wife... now my wife is
taking a nap while I'm

writing my travels take..
my eyes are tire and I
must stop writing for now
of cause many more my
travels take later....,
Now the plane flying
higher to avoid the storm
heaviest win down below...
sky begins to look likes
drift likes mixing with smal
shower.. the beauty of
whiteness of whitnessof
sky still remain there

licking getting and death
and that is the life nature
said Buddha... and it is
real apply to all life on
earth,,,

... A life under the sun is
the nickname of the
beautiful Fot
Landerdale ... in Fl...

....

Stat 5:6 captain

Chapter 18

A Brief Biography of Sommai Suesattaya

Sommai Suesattaya was a relative and considered the younger brother of Uncle Inpuk, also known as Intrakiat (Thongin) Rodpradit. Around 1961–1963, Uncle Inpuk entrusted him to Phra Maha Thamongkham Dhammasaro of Wat Mai Phiren, Pho Sam Ton, Thonburi, so he could pursue his secondary education at Taweethapisek School, a renowned high school near Wat Arun (Temple of Dawn).

Starting as a temple boy, Sommai later graduated with a degree in engineering from King Mongkut's Institute of Technology Ladkrabang and earned a master's degree in the same field from Chulalongkorn University. He secured a stable career at the Department of Highways, where he held the position of chief engineer, achieving significant success in his professional life. After retiring from government service, he was invited to serve as a consultant for a major construction company, a role he continued to fulfill until the final days of his life.

Born in Phetchabun Province on December 25, 1952, to father Jaran Suy and mother Bua Pa Suesattaya, Sommai had a total of eight siblings. He was the eldest child. He married Mrs. Wipa Suesattaya (Thamnao), but they had no children together.

He graduated from Phothi Phitthaya Phayak School in high school and earned a Bachelor's degree in Civil Engineering from King Mongkut's Institute of Technology Ladkrabang. He also obtained a Master's degree in Structural Engineering from Chulalongkorn University. He received his professional engineering license from the Engineering Institute of Thailand."He began his government service at the Analysis and Research Division of the Department of Highways as a Civil Engineer 3. He worked in the Survey and Design Division of the Department of Highways, specifically in the Chachoengsao area at Sriracha. He held the position of Director of the Survey and Design Section of the 3rd Highway Office (Sakon Nakhon) and later served as the Director of the Survey and Design Section of the 7th Highway Office (Ubon Ratchathani). He was also appointed as the Director of the Planning Section of the 12th Highway Office (Chonburi) until his retirement.

After retiring from government service, he worked with several consulting companies, eventually joining Chotjinda Consultant Co., Ltd., specializing in safety, until the end of his career. On December 6, 2024, he was hospitalized at Somdet Phra Pin Klao Hospital, Navy Department, due to diarrhea and fatigue. He passed away peacefully at 07:40 AM. He was 75 years old at the time of his passing."

Dr.Sompong (Daney) Dumdeang is a former Law Professor of the University of Washington, United States of America, and is currently a Real-estate Investor in USA.has sent his letter of condolence to Sommai's family:

So long friendship

I do know Nong Sommai way back over 50 years, plus we lived in Wat Maipiren, Dhonburi. We, Thong In myself, Sommai, and Nong Prapas, are more than friends but family friends. We always keep in touch even though I live in the U.S.A.. Nong Sommai in Thailand., but we keep in touch closely. Last I saw him a few years, about 8 years ago, the year I conducted my research in Khao Khlo of Petchaboon Province where Sommai and his wife together with Nong Prapas and his wife, and we celebrated our reunion in Khao Khlo, and we have a such a warmest friendship times, no words to speech.

I am too shocked to lose him... He is an ongoing person, polite about others, making others smile, and always doing new things.

Sommai was a diligent and hardworking person, always eager to learn new things both in the worldly and spiritual aspects.

In his work, Sommai carried out his duties with honesty and integrity, showing an exceptional sense of responsibility toward his tasks. He had a kind and compassionate nature, loved his colleagues, and was respectful toward his superiors. He was courteous to the elderly and always demonstrated great kindness throughout his long career, fully dedicating himself to his responsibilities.

His physical strength, mental determination, and intelligence were devoted to working for the benefit of the nation, which is immeasurable.

In terms of religion, he had great faith in Buddhism and continuously supported and nurtured the Buddhist faith.

In the family, he was highly grateful and showed great reverence. He performed his duties as the head of the family excellently, always caring for and supporting his siblings. He was a good life partner to his wife, providing warmth and happiness to the family. Sommai was an optimist, always looking at the world with a positive perspective.

See you in heaven.

Your older brother,

P, Daney Dumdeang

Uncle Inpook" exchanged opinions via LINE with "Dr. Sompong Damdaeng" while Dr. Sompong Damdaeng attended Sommai's funeral in Phanat Nikhom.

It's not just me who admires the spirit of a friend who always does for others. Both Nong Jan and Luk Dech appreciate and highly praise our friend for his attentiveness and sacrifices in coming to attend Sommai's funeral, even though he still had to fly south to take care of his younger sister, Nong Ubon Damdaeng's funeral on December 10, 2024. Initially, I informed my friend that I might not be able to attend Sommai's funeral because I couldn't find a way to come, as I felt hesitant about leaving my children. Nong Jan, my daughter, had already taken several days off because she was sent by her office to attend a science seminar in New Orleans for just five days. However, she took the opportunity to travel and relax in the United States for almost three weeks, which limited her available leave time. But when she learned that our friend had attended Sommai's funeral, they were both willing to request time off from their work to meet and see our friend.

Thank you. And on the occasion of the funeral of Nong Sommai, Mr. Weera Suesat, or Nong Weerasak Satyatheeranon, President of the Council of Rajabhat University Sisaket, wrote the following on his Facebook:

Sometimes, in moments of regret, there is also some goodness that we encounter. We meet relatives, close friends, and companions whom we haven't seen in a long time. If it weren't for such an event, the chance of meeting again would be quite rare. The two people standing and holding the burial cloth...

In the first image on the left, he had once been ordained as a novice at Wat Mai Phiren, Isarap Road, Bangkok Yai District, Bangkok. After disrobing, the first person, Dr. Sompong Dumdeang (the dark-skinned person), originally from Ranod, Songkhla Province, received a Fulbright scholarship to study in the United States and graduated with a Ph.D. He now resides in Oregon, USA. Currently, he is 79 years old.

Here's the translation:

The second person, Uncle Thong-in or Uncle In-Puk, or Intharakiet Rodpradit, after disrobing, went on to study in the Philippines.

He later worked at Kasikorn Bank and retired from working at a French bank.

He currently lives with his daughter in Bangkok. Uncle In-Puk is 82 years old and was born in Ban Non Muang, Nong Muang Subdistrict, Borabu District, Maha Sarakham Province. I am glad to have met both of them.

Uncle In-Puk took a photo with Prosecutor Veerasak Satyathiranon on December 10, 2024.

Prosecutor Veerasak offered a burial cloth.

175

Uncle Inpook took a photo with Prosecutor Veerasak and the siblings of the late Sommai."

Feel free to ask if you'd like further adjustments!

Prosecutor Veerasak takes a photo with Dr. Sompong Dumdeang and the senior
relatives of the deceased.

Loy Angkarn

Dr. Sompong Damdaeng took a photo with the relatives of the deceased.

Uncle Inpuk offered the funeral cloth together with Dr. Sompong Damdaeng from the United States.

Prosecutor Virasakdi presided jointly with Dr. Sompong Damdaeng in the chanting ceremony for the deceased.

Personal Philosophy
Reflections on Life
Thoughts on Life
Author's Philosophy

Nothing is certain in life.
What can be big can also be small.
What can be rich can also become poor.
What can be strong can also become sick.

Life is impermanent

Impermanent is the body, it's never steady,
It cannot escape, change, or sway away.
Death will come, to both man and woman,
For death is given to everyone today.

In times of hardship, what remains are deeds,
The good and bad that one has done everywhere.
Therefore, I warn my fellow humans, all living beings,
To live with goodness before it's too late.
Follow the words of the wise, discard the evil,
Do not stray or become trapped in pride.
If we worship the Triple Gem,
We will surely find our way to the heavenly realm.
If we miss that, we will still be in Nirvana, the eternal realm,
And if we miss Nirvana, we will still enjoy heaven with peace.
If we miss heaven, we will be born human,
And find great joy and relief.
We will not encounter the endless cycle of suffering.
(Three Novices, WongSathorn Timklip)

With mindfulness, remember and pay attention to the teachings of the Buddha. In short, it can be understood as:

Four bearers: The four elements—earth, water, wind, and fire.
Three followers: Impermanence, suffering, and non-self.
One person sitting on the chair: The mind.
Two leading figures: Karma, both good and bad.

ile alive, we are caught in endless turmoil.
When we become a corpse, lifeless and still.
The cycle of samsara is clear, all is truthful.
Everything is impermanent, it cannot endure.

Wealth and possessions circulate, changing owners.
The body must part, despite its resistance.
Born and then perishing, fading away, never to return.
Hasten to awaken from delusion and worldly attachment.

Create good deeds, store up the fruits of merit.
No matter how many lifetimes, may fortune find you.
May happiness be complete and ever-increasing,
For good deeds provide the foundation for prosperity.

If you look at a corpse, see it as a corpse.
Calm the mind, for the body is nature, teaching truth.
The corpse teaches us to reduce and abandon desires,
For persistence in craving leads to confusion and suffering.

The future is uncertain, just like this.
It is unstable, shifting, always slipping away.
Do good uphold virtue before it fades.
When life ends, there will be no regret, for we lived as humans.

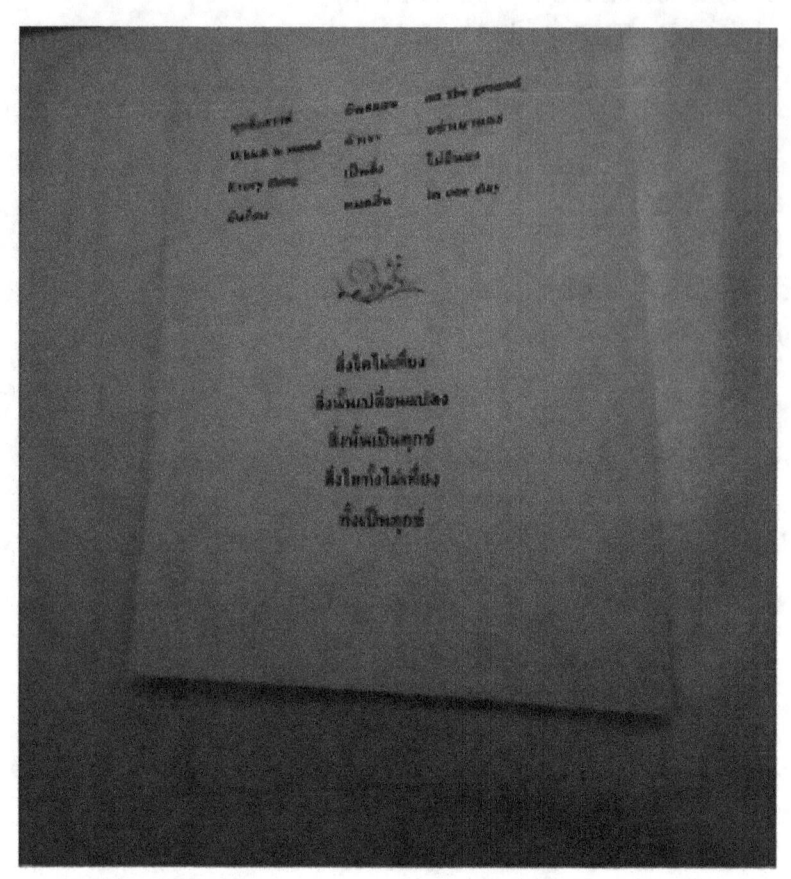

Dr.Sompong Daney Dumdeang,

President,

(Dumdeang Foundation,)

933 S.E.Reynolds Street, Portland, Oregon, 97202, USA.

In Loving Memory of the Reverend Chao Khun

Sympathy note to Phra Pariyatti Kosol or Arjarn Chao Khun Sathiarn, the Abbot of Wat Maipirin, Thonburi.

งานเลี้ยงฯที่.จ.เพชรบุรี./7/12/2567...

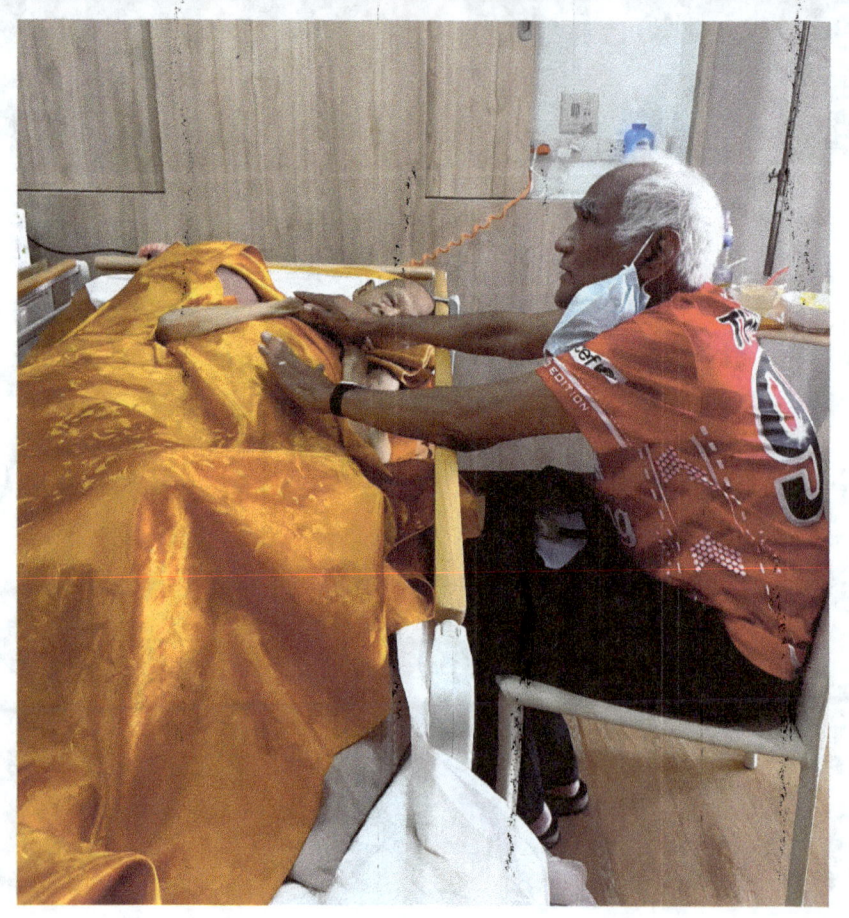

I was so super shocked and crying when I read a message from P. Chin saying that Arjarn Sathien had passed away. My body felt like it was falling down, and I cried. My wife asked me what was happening. I said, "Arjarn Sathien passed away yesterday." I was in shock, and my wife hugged me. I said, "I'm so sorry, honey."

She said, "I'm glad you saw him last week. He said thank you for visiting him. He told you he had enough medicine. Good luck, Look Maha Pong. He is happy in heaven, honey," said my wife.

Later, I read the messages from Nong Art, Nong Thawee, and others about the sad news of Arjarn Sathien's passing. I was still in a state of shock—speechless—sitting in my hotel room, praying for him during that quiet, emotional moment. I read a sympathy note from Khun Thong Intr... and I felt a little better, because Arjarn Sathien was a monk for everyone—for us, for the government, for the nation. He did more than we could ever imagine. His actions were louder than words.

I am one of those whom he supported from the beginning all the way to where I am now.

I am so sorry that I could not come to participate in his holy shower bath ceremony because of my tight schedule—going from one NBE to the next nonstop. However, I'm glad I visited him before. He recognized me, and we had a great conversation together. That was our final meeting, and we shared a meaningful conversation.

It was a miracle—indescribable for me.

He is in heaven now, with all the good deeds he did for us. He is resting in peace now.

We all celebrate his new life.

A Tribute in Honor of Chao Khun Phra Piriya Kosol
Venerable Ajahn Sathian Chantako
Abbot of Wat Mai Piren, Thonburi

Nothing in life is guaranteed.
One can rise, and one can fall.
Wealth can turn to poverty.
Health can give way to illness.

(Life is impermanent)

Impermanent are all formations,
No way to escape, no deviations.
Death approaches both woman and man,
For none can outrun its final span.

In times of misfortune, only good and bad remain,
For all that one has done, in every domain.
Thus, I urge all fellow beings, in every life and form,
To live with goodness, before the storm.
Hold fast to the words of wisdom, and be aware,
Do not wander in pride, lost in despair.

If we live reverently, worshipping the Triple Gem,
Upon decision, we'll find the heavenly realm.
If we falter, Nibbana, the immortal land,
We'll still enjoy heaven's joy, at its command.
f heaven is missed, as humans we'll delight,
We'll avoid the realms of suffering and plight.
(From the novice monk, Wongsathon Timklip)

With mindfulness, remember and pay attention to the teachings of the Buddha. In short, it can be understood as:

1. **Four bearers**: The four elements—earth, water, wind, and fire.

2. **Three followers**: Impermanence, suffering, and non-self.

194

3. **One person sitting on the chair**: The mind.

4. **Two leading figures**: Karma, both good and bad.

When alive, there is chaos, never-ending,
But when dead, the body lies still, no more contending.
The cycle of existence is clear, truthful and true,
All things are impermanent, nothing stays through.

Wealth and possessions revolve, changing hands,
The body must part, despite all its demands.
Born and then perishing, fading away, never to return,
Awaken quickly from delusion, from worldly concerns.

Create merit and accumulate the results of good deeds,
No matter how many lifetimes, they will bring prosperity indeed.
Happiness, smooth and complete, will increase and grow,
For doing good acts will serve as your foundation, bestow.

If you look at a corpse, you will see a corpse,
A calm mind sees it as a teaching, a truth that brings forth.
The corpse teaches us to reduce and abandon,
Desire and effort lead only to confusion and ruin.

In the future, we too shall be like this,
Unstable, drifting, waiting to fade and miss.
Do good deeds, live with virtue before you decay,
When you pass, you won't regret having been human in your way.

Dr.Sompong Daney Dumdeang,

President,

(Dumdeang Foundation,)

933 S.E.Reynolds Street, Portland, Oregon, 97202, USA.

Chapter 19

The biography of Phra Rajaburiyatikosol

เกิด	๑๒ กันยายน พ.ศ. ๒๔๗๑
อายุ	๙๓ ปี
อุปสมบท	๑๐ มิถุนายน พ.ศ. ๒๔๙๑
พรรษา	๗๔
วัด	วัดใหม่พิเรนทร์
ท้องที่	กรุงเทพมหานคร
สังกัด	มหานิกาย
วุฒิการ	น.ธ.เอก, ป.ธ.๙
ศึกษา	

The person who played a key role in bringing the writer to Wat Mai Phiren and meeting Phra Rajaburiyatikosol was the writer's boxing teacher, Nimit Luedmuangtai. In addition to teaching the writer Thai boxing while the writer was studying in high school, Nimit Luedmuangtai was also a relative of the writer. When Nimit Luedmuangtai came to Bangkok to fight in boxing and gained fame in the Thai boxing industry, he wanted to support and help the writer have a better future. He encouraged the writer to continue studying in Bangkok. The writer decided to travel by train, and Nimit Luedmuangtai was the one who picked the writer up at Hua Lamphong Station. Afterward, Nimit took the writer to meet Mahawit Settha Sawat, an upperclassman from Wat Hua Pom in Mueang District, Songkhla Province. Mahawit was the grandson of Master Maha Somphong Maneephrom, who was a relative of Master Maha Prasit Busabong. Master Maha Prasit Busabong was one of the first senior monks from Southern Thailand who resided at Wat Mai Phiren. He was close and held great respect for Nimit Luedmuangtai. However, when Nimit Luedmuangtai took the writer to meet and leave the writer with Master Maha Prasit, Master Maha Prasit was not available. Instead, Phra Maha Setthi Chanthako, or Phra Rajaburiyatikosol, was the one who accepted the writer.

Phra Rajaburiyatikosol had previously stayed in the southern region before moving to Bangkok. His last residence in the south was at Wat Chong Klang, Ching Sae Sub-district, Ranod District, Songkhla Province, in 1947. He then moved to stay at Wat Mai Phiren, Wat Arun Sub-district, Bang Kho Laem District, Bangkok, on May 10, 1957.

Phra Rajaburiyatikosol, Master Setthien, was a monk with great diligence and perseverance. He passed the Pali examination for six levels in 1965 at the Satun Santiaram Temple School, Piman Sub-district, Mueang District, Satun Province. Later, he passed the nine-level Pali examination, which is the highest level of education for Thai monks, while residing at Wat Mai Phiren, Wat Arun Sub-district, Bang Kho Laem District, and studying at the Wat Mai Phiren Religious Studies Institute and Wat Arun Rajwararam School in Bangkok in 1991. Having passed the six levels and then waiting 26 years to achieve the nine levels is a remarkable record of perseverance that no one has yet achieved, as Master Setthien did.

The author, together with the disciples, collected gifts to offer on the occasion of the birthday of Phra Maha Setthien (Chanthako) Rattanasuwan at Wat Mai Phiren and wished for the teacher's good health, that he may continue to uphold his monastic vows as a refuge for the disciples and laypeople for many more years. They also prayed for him to pass the Pali examination for the ninth level. It can be said that the request from the disciples, combined with his high level of perseverance, led him to never give up on his studies. Despite his age, he did not let it be a barrier to his efforts, and eventually, he passed the Pali examination for the ninth level, fulfilling the wishes of his disciples and lay supporters. In addition to his study of Pali according to the Thai monk education system and achieving the ninth-level Pali examination, Master Setthien also passed the advanced teacher qualification examination under the Ministry of Education (P.M.).

Phra Maha Setthien was appointed as the abbot of Wat Mai Phiren, Wat Arun, Bangkok Yai District, Bangkok, on May 15, 1991, succeeding Phra Kru Prawit Vihara, the 7th abbot. After taking on the role, he diligently performed various religious duties. He became the first Phra Ratcha Khen (Royal Monk) of Wat Mai Phiren, receiving the royal graciousness from His Majesty the King, who conferred the title 'Phra Sri Rattana Simon' in 1999. Since then, he has dedicated himself fully to serving the Sangha, both in the temple's internal and external religious duties, earning the trust and respect of the senior clergy and the Sangha. He was later honored with the title 'Phra Priyatikosol' and was granted the royal fanhood of office by His Majesty King Maha Vajiralongkorn, at the Amarindra Winitchai Throne Hall in the Grand Palace, Bangkok, on December 5, 2007.

พระราชปริยัติโกศล (เสถียร ฐานโต ป.ธ.๙)

As a former close disciple of the Venerable Master, the author presents a brief summary of the works of Phra Rajapariyattikosol as follows:

The work on the development of the temple's infrastructure.

As the assistant abbot, Venerable Phra Rajabhirakosol (Sethian) played a key role in assisting Phra Kru Prawit Wihara in the construction of various buildings in the temple, ensuring their orderly arrangement. He helped build 10 sturdy brick buildings, and continued to oversee the construction of several more structures during his tenure as the abbot, which continues to this day.

Educational work

Venerable Acharn Setthian saw that the development of various structures and facilities had reached an adequate level, so he focused on human development. He emphasized providing opportunities, scholarships, love, compassion, and encouragement so that individuals could become good, knowledgeable people. With knowledge, they could uphold themselves, protect the nation, and preserve the Dharma. As he once said: 'Every person has their good qualities. It's impossible for anyone to be entirely bad. We must provide opportunities and compassion, for only then will they develop into good members of society.'

It is clear that, under the administration of Venerable Acharn Setthian, the education system in both the Dharma and Pali departments, as well as worldly studies, succeeded in producing monks in the Wat Mai Phiren school who passed the Pali examinations, achieving up to 9 levels of Pali scholarship with 6 monks achieving the highest ranking. This is the largest number ever seen. In addition, in terms of worldly studies, many monks were encouraged to pursue higher education, even obtaining doctoral degrees. This is an outstanding achievement that brought great recognition and fame to Wat Mai Phiren.

Work in the Promotion of the Dharma

Venerable Acharn sent capable monks with experience in teaching and advanced studies to manage religious affairs in various provinces, as well as to spread the Dharma abroad, including in Europe, America, and India.

Work in Sermons

Venerable Acharn Setthian has been continuously engaged in training and teaching both monks and laypeople, delivering numerous Dharma talks. One of the most significant ones, which the writer found particularly interesting, was the talk on 'Matapitu-Khun Katha' (The Gratitude towards Parents). This is significant because, during the time when the writer was still a monk at Wat Mai Phiren, he was invited to deliver a sermon on 'Gratitude and Duty towards Parents,' which was in harmony with Venerable Acharn's sermon. The writer has preached on this topic multiple times, both in Songkhla and at Wat Mai Phiren."

And it was well received by the laypeople. The writer wishes to present the Dharma sermon of Venerable Acharn and summarize his teachings on 'Matapitu-Khun Katha' (The Gratitude toward Parents) for the readers as follows:

'In Buddhism, the Buddha highly honors parents who provide care and support to their children, considering them in the highest regard. Parents who care for their children are revered as Brahma, as the first teachers, and are to be respected and honored by their children.

The high esteem the Buddha places on parents can be explained as follows:

Parents are considered to be Brahma to their children. The term "Brahma" refers to the creator of the world and all things, the supreme deity according to Brahmanism. The reason the Buddha praises parents as Brahma to their children is that parents possess four divine qualities:

1. **Metta (Loving-kindness)**: The love and good wishes parents have for their children, desiring their happiness.

2. **Karuna (Compassion)**: The sorrow and desire to help their children escape from suffering.

3. **Mudita (Sympathetic joy)**: The joy parents feel when their children succeed and are happy.

(4) **Upekkha (Equanimity)**: This refers to a state of balanced, calm, and impartial observation, where a parent maintains peace of mind when their child is capable of taking responsibility for their actions or when the child deserves the consequences of their actions.

Parents are considered **Bhurpajaaraya (First Teachers)** for their children because they teach them through words and actions. They instruct their children on how to behave, what to say, and how to interact with others. Parents guide their children on what is appropriate behavior, thus serving as their first teachers.

Parents are also referred to as **Aahuneyya** (worthy of veneration). This term signifies that parents deserve the highest respect, like revered saints. Parents are selfless in their compassion and kindness toward their children, forgiving their mistakes and always wishing them well. Even when their children falter, parents still desire their children's happiness and success.

As children, recognizing the great merits of our parents reminds us of the importance of gratitude, which is a marker of goodness, as expressed in the proverb, "Nimit Tang Sāthu rūpānaṅ, Kattān'yu kattuweṭhita," which emphasizes that gratitude and reverence are signs of a virtuous person.

The phrase **"Gratitude and Repayment"** is composed of two words: **"Gratitude"** and **"Repayment."**

- **"Gratitude"** means "Grateful" or "Recognizing the value of someone's kindness." It refers to acknowledging the gratitude and kindness of those who have helped us.

- **"Repayment"** means "Repayment" or "Reciprocation," the act of repaying or returning the favor of someone's kindness.

Thus, the phrase **"Gratitude and Repayment"** refers to the quality of being grateful and reciprocating kindness, especially through acts of paying back or honoring the benefactor. It's often compared to "true gold," showing that a genuinely good person proves their goodness by caring for and honoring their parents.

Five ways to repay the kindness of one's parents (according to Buddhist teachings):

1. **Repay the care given** – This means that children should care for their parents as the parents once cared for them. This includes providing for their well-being and ensuring their comfort in both physical and emotional aspects.

2. **Assist with their work** – Children should help lighten the burden of their parents' duties and tasks. If the child is still young, this means focusing on their studies instead of adding more stress to the parents' responsibilities.

3. **Preserve the family lineage** – This involves maintaining the wealth and values passed down by the parents, ensuring they don't fall into ruin. If the parents live a virtuous life, the child should also follow their example, adhering to good principles or even guiding their parents back to righteousness if they have strayed.

4. **Conduct oneself appropriately as an heir**: This means that children should behave according to the guidance and teachings of their parents, who raised them with love and good intentions. Children should not go astray or behave dishonorably, as the hopes of their parents are placed upon them.

5. **After they have passed, perform merit-making for them**: This refers to the natural course of life, where everyone is subject to birth, aging, sickness, and death. When parents pass away, children should arrange proper funeral rites fitting their parents' status and consistently dedicate merit to them.

The Buddha also made an analogy, saying, "If a child were to carry the mother on their right shoulder and the father on their left, supporting them, feeding them, and caring for their needs, even if they lived to be 100 years old and served them their whole life, it would still not be enough to repay their kindness."

As the Buddha said, "Mātāpitu upaṭṭhānaṃ etaṃ maṅkala muttamaṃ," which translates to "The care of one's parents is the highest of all blessings."

The author has always held great respect for the revered monk. Despite having settled in the United States for many years, the author, along with his wife, Patty, always makes it a point to visit the monk and pay their respects whenever they return to their hometown. The image shows one such occasion.

This passage reflects the deep reverence and cultural importance of maintaining spiritual ties, regardless of where one lives. It highlights the author's commitment to honoring long-held traditions and showing respect to a respected figure in their life.

In 2018, the clergy, laypeople, and disciples of the revered monk organized a ceremony to celebrate his 90th birthday. As mentioned by the monks of Wat Mai Phiren, the temple is an ancient one with a long history. It has contributed significantly to both the community and the Buddhist faith. The temple's abbot played a key role in driving change and development, leading to the improvements seen today. The current abbot, Phra Ratchapariyathikosol (Setthian Chanta Ko, Ph.D. 9), has continued the work of developing the temple over several decades, working alongside the clergy, laypeople, and devout supporters of the temple.

Creating happiness and benefits, overcoming numerous obstacles and challenges.

In 2019, the year marking the 90th birthday of Phra Ratcha Phariyathokosal, a key figure at Wat Mai Phiren, the celebration was an auspicious event. His strong health and longevity were celebrated by the monks, laypeople, and disciples alike. In response to the news, everyone united to organize a merit-making ceremony to honor him, offering encouragement and gratitude. It was a meaningful occasion to enhance good deeds and express appreciation.

The author, who is a close disciple, felt happiness and pride that the teacher was in such good health at the age of 90. However, the author, involved in voluntary work in the United States, could not attend the celebration. Instead, the author sent a message of respect and joy, asking a dear friend, Intharakit Rodpradit, to represent them at the event. Intharakit, a fellow disciple, was also a co-author of the book *The Crisis of Conflict in the Three Southern Border Provinces.*

The teacher also allowed a close meeting.

The philosophy of Venerable Phra Rajabhirakosol

Being a monk, one must be content with little and live simply. Make oneself easy to live with, easy to feed, eat just enough to be satisfied, be content with what one has, and be happy with what one can attain. When it's time to sleep, don't bring work or problems into your thoughts to cause stress (work is for work, sleep is for rest).

The author would like to dedicate a poem on gratitude to Venerable Phra Rajabhirakosol and to all readers as follows:

"Gratitude" – three words, easy to remember,
But their meaning is deep, vast beyond measure.
The important virtues, six in total,
Should be embraced and firmly kept in the heart.

The greatest of all, first and foremost, are father and mother,
They share their love and kindness, immense and boundless.
We should honor them with care, above all else,
And show concern and gratitude for them throughout our lives.

The land, the birthplace,
We must exalt and honor it until our last breath.
When enemies invade, we must defend it with courage,
Ready to fight and protect the land.

Religion, a refuge, we must bow and worship,
Never allowing anyone to defile or trespass upon it.
We must follow the Buddha's teachings,
Upholding the principles of dharma and discipline.

The Sovereign – is the king, a noble ruler,
He is the supreme leader, every era,
A source of joy for the kingdom, a guiding beacon,
One should uphold loyalty, be devoted and true.

Remember the teacher,
Who guided and taught,
eflect on their kindness, more than just duties,
Even when parting, leaving this world for many years,
We offer homage, engraving it in the heart.

To all those who supported,
And helped us along the way,
Repay their kindness, never let it slip away,
Show respect and gratitude to everyone,
May the good deeds return, reflected back to you.

Even with six, gratitude is fully practiced,
Following the customs without resistance.
Joy brings lasting results,
Smooth happiness when holding firmly to "Gratitude".

With the utmost respect, I humbly pay homage to the esteemed teacher,
From the past, Maha Sompong Damdaeng.
Dr. Sompong Damdaeng,
President of the Damdaeng Foundation.

(Dumdeang Foundation)

933 SE.Renolds Street, Portland, Oregon, 97202, USA.

Chapter 20

Moo Deng

"Moo Deng" is a nickname for a female pygmy hippopotamus living in Khao Kheow Open Zoo in Chonburi, Thailand. The name "Moo Deng" (which translates to "Bouncing Pig") became popular after an image of the animal went viral on the internet in September 2024, turning it into an internet meme. It is known for its cuteness and the playful nature captured in the viral image.

The author has arrived in Thailand to meet Moo Deng, as I have been informed by Tom, my assistant. Moo Deng is shocking the world with the news of her unique characteristic, which has attracted tourists from around the world to Thailand, greatly boosting the country's popularity and increasing the revenue of the nation's tourism industry by millions of dollars.

Thanks to Moo Deng being born in Thailand and becoming a superstar among animal lovers, the author, as an animal lover himself, has his own foundation for his pets named Merley, Boo Boo, Rama, Pata, and Ok Styaitown Sammyanda. HH is the late animal foundation.

Moo Deng is a pygmy hippo living in Khao Kheow Open Zoo in Thailand, who gained notability in September 2024 as a popular Internet meme after images of her went viral online. Because of the popularity of the hippo, whose name translates to «bouncy pork," the zoo saw a boosted attendance. It has been reported that some visitors to the zoo threw water and other objects at the baby hippo to get her to react.

Several folktales have been collected about the pygmy hippopotamus. One tale says that pygmy hippos carry a shining diamond in their mouths to help travel through thick forests at night; by day, the pygmy hippo has a secret hiding place for the diamond, but if a hunter catches a pygmy hippo at night, the diamond can be taken. Villagers sometimes believed that baby pygmy hippos do not nurse but rather lick secretions off the skin of the mother.

Moo Deng was born on July 10, 2024, to parents Tony and Jona. The name 'Moo Deng' was chosen through a public voting process, with over 20,000 people voting for the name. Moo Deng has six siblings, including Moo Tun, a pygmy hippopotamus who is also popular at Khao Kheow Open Zoo.

Moo Deng was born on July 10, 2024, to parents Tony and Jona. The name 'Moo Deng' was chosen through a public voting process, with more than 20,000 people voting for the name. "Moo Deng has six older siblings." As well as Moo Toon Which is also a popular pygmy hippopotamus at Khao Kheow Open Zoo.

Popular news about bouncing pigs in September A.D. 2567

Khao Kheow Open Zoo posted a picture of Moo Deng on their Facebook page. Officially, it quickly became a favorite. Moo Deng is known for being more cheerful and energetic than other pygmy hippos. In response to Moo Deng's popularity, Khao Kheow Open Zoo announced that they would be selling clothing and other souvenir items designed based on Moo Deng. In addition, a coffee shop has produced a realistic cake shaped like Moo Deng. In Japan, fan art images have been posted. In Japan, fan art inspired by Moo Deng has been posted on X[1]. Moreover, various products and services have incorporated Moo Deng into their advertisements and promotional campaigns, Including GMM Music, a subsidiary of GMM Grammy. Which released a song about Moo Deng in 4 languages, including Thai, English, Chinese, and Japanese.

Moo Deng's appearance at the 29th National Book Fair.

Due to the rapid spread of Moo Deng's popularity on the internet, the daily number of visitors to the zoo has doubled, especially on September 7th and 8th, 2024, when the total number of visitors exceeded ten thousand people. However, some tourists harassed Moo Deng by splashing water at her. And threw objects at her to make her react. The staff at Khao Kheow Open Zoo then installed security cameras around the enclosure, and the zoo director announced that they would take legal action against tourists who harassed Moo Deng. The behavior was widely condemned on the internet. Later, the zoo limited the visiting time for Moo Deng to five minutes per person to accommodate the increasing number of tourists.

211

212

213

Chapter 21

Journey to heaven that never return to earth

Twenty children dead after Thailand school bus fire

1 October 2024

BBC News

Reuters Firefighters work to extinguish a burned-out school busReuters

The bus, carrying dozens of primary school-age children, was returning from a trip north of Bangkok

The bodies of 20 children and three teachers have been recovered after a bus transporting school pupils crashed and caught fire outside Bangkok.

The bus was returning to the Thai capital after a school trip to the north of the country.

Videos from the scene showed flames engulfing the bus as it burned under an overpass, with huge clouds of dense black smoke billowing into the sky.

The driver handed himself into police 100km (61 miles) north of Bangkok, according to local media.

Getty Images A relative of a student who died in a bus fire covers the eyes of a young relative as they walk past the wreckage of the bus Getty Images.

Distraught loved ones of people killed in the tragedy visited the crash site.

Footage taken shortly after the fatal crash showed the driver attempting to extinguish the fire, but he reportedly fled the scene.

Witnesses say the bus crashed into the concrete barrier dividing the highway just north of Bangkok after a front tire burst.

The bus was quickly consumed by an intense fire, and many on board were unable to get out. The cause of the fire is still unknown.

Nineteen children and three teachers are reported to have survived, sixteen of whom are being treated in hospital for their injuries.

Reuters Firefighters transfer bodies from a burnt-out bus that was carrying teachers and students from Wat Khao Phraya school, Reuters.

Firefighters remove a wrapped-up body from the bus

Transport Minister Suriyahe Juangroongruangkit said the bus was powered by "extremely risky" compressed natural gas.

"This is a very tragic incident," Mr Suriyahe told reporters at the scene.

"The ministry must find a measure... if possible, for passenger vehicles like this to be banned from using this type of fuel because it's extremely risky."

Piyalak Thinkaew, who was leading the search, said it was hard to identify the bodies because they were so badly burnt.

"Some of the bodies we found were very, very small," he told reporters at the scene, adding that the fire started at the front of the bus.

"The kids' instinct was to escape to the back so the bodies were there," he said.

Forensic police said of the 23 bodies found, eleven were male, seven female and a further five were unidentifiable.

Getty Images A police officer inspects a burnt-out bus that was carrying students and teachers on the outskirts of Bangkok on October 1, 2024. Rescuers pulled children's bodies from the charred wreckage of a Thai school bus on October 1 after an accident turned the vehicle into an inferno, with more than 20 feared dead.Getty Images

Rescuers pulled children's bodies from the charred wreckage

The ages of the children on board remains unclear, but the school caters for pupils between three and 15 years old.

Thailand has one of the worst road safety records in the world, with unsafe vehicles and poor driving contributing to roughly 20,000 fatalities a year.

Thailand's Deputy Prime Minister, Anutin Charnvirakul, said an investigation was underway. "We have to investigate the trace of driving from the tire marks, the burning trace, and CCTV footage," he said.

Thai forensic police officers inspect a burnt bus on Vibhavadi Rangsit road in Bangkok, Thailand, 01 October 2024.

Could the deaths of 20 school children help make Thailand's roads safer?

Investigators found a series of safety failures following the accident, leaving the country shocked.

A tragic incident has occurred on Vibhavadi Rangsit Road, where a fire broke out on a school bus. Initial reports indicate that seven people have died. The total number of individuals on the bus, including students and teachers, is 44. Of these, 19 were able to escape the fire, while 25 remain unaccounted for and are waiting for identification verification. The authorities are investigating the cause of the fire and working on identifying the missing persons.

A tragic incident occurred on Vibhavadi Rangsit Road at 12:20 PM, where a school bus caught fire. The fire broke out opposite Phahonyothin 72. Details of the casualties and investigation are still being confirmed, but the situation has resulted in several fatalities, with efforts underway to identify missing individuals.

Initial reports indicate that the bus involved in the fire was a school bus from Uthai Thani Province, carrying students on an educational trip. While the exact number of casualties and injuries is still under investigation, emergency responders managed to contain the fire. The situation is still being examined for further details. (Image and information from Fire & Rescue Thailand's Facebook page)

aomaom_kanyarat 📷 🌐
15h

สวยมากเลยค่ะ😍😍🧡🧡

377

1

19

Send

219

220

Most relevant ⌄

ชีพสุมล ศรีวิเชียร
ขอให้คุณครูเดินทางไปสู่
สรวงสวรรค์โดยสวัสดิภาพนะ
คะพร้อมเด็กๆทั้ง20คนและ
คุณครูอีกสองท่าน

228

Chapter 22

Christmas in Thailand

We had planned to go to Thailand on a family trip in December. But I received bad news—my younger sister, Ubon Dumdeang, passed away suddenly. So, I left early on the twenty-fourth of November 2024 to honor and pay my last respects to my sister.

The rest of the group followed me two weeks later on different flights at different times.

When I returned home, people in America asked, "How was your trip to Thailand?" I had the hardest time answering, truly.

Why? Because it was a mix of both joy and sadness. If I hadn't lost my sister, this trip would have been an excellent one—well-organized, well-managed, and full of amazing adventures. We solved problems within the group quickly, handled any miscommunication immediately, and supported each other emotionally, financially, and physically. It was just the best group of travelers—from Portland to Vancouver, from Canada to Bangkok, from Bangkok to Chiang Mai, from Chiang Mai to Krabi International Airport, and from Krabi to Li Pe. We traveled from the north to the south of Thailand, making this an unforgettable journey.

We celebrated Christmas in Li Pe, making it a truly special Thailand Christmas. One thing I learned from group travel is how to handle conflicts when they arise, how to help each other when someone falls sick, how to adjust schedules, and how to save money together while traveling. Most importantly, we looked out for each other's health and safety.

Our group was the best of the best—traveling together as a family in 2024.

This book serves as a guide, helping readers learn how to embrace and enjoy every moment with one another. No matter where you travel in the world, the true value of the journey comes from investing time, money, and friendship into shared experiences. Through adventure, challenges, and discovery in foreign lands, we learn not only about new places but also about life and each other.

Southern trips

Tourism

Ko Lipe has three main beaches: Sunset Beach (*Hat Pramong*), Sunrise Beach (*Hat Chao Ley*), and Pattaya Beach. The calm, clear water makes Ko Lipe ideal for snorkeling, with 25 percent of the world's tropical fish species found in the area.

Ko Lipe is also popular with Generation X and typically older generations looking for a peaceful break.

Activity

Popular activities for visitors to the island include sightseeing of natural features, water sports such as scuba diving, snorkeling, and kayaking, boat trips to nearby islands and reefs such as Ko Usen and Ko Kra, and dining—particularly fresh seafood on Walking Street.

Visitors take in sunrise views on Sunrise Beach and partake in nightlife on Pattaya Beach.

Scuba diving and snorkeling around Ko Lipe are often viewed as some of the best in Thailand because of the healthy reefs and the range of marine life.

UNFORGETTABLE

Legends say that hummingbirds float free of time, carrying our hopes for love, joy and celebration. The hummingbird's delicate grace reminds us that life is rich, beauty is everywhere, every personal connection has meaning and that laughter is life's sweetest creation.

Morgan Allen Middal
Sunrise
May 22, 1974
Sunset
March 27, 2012

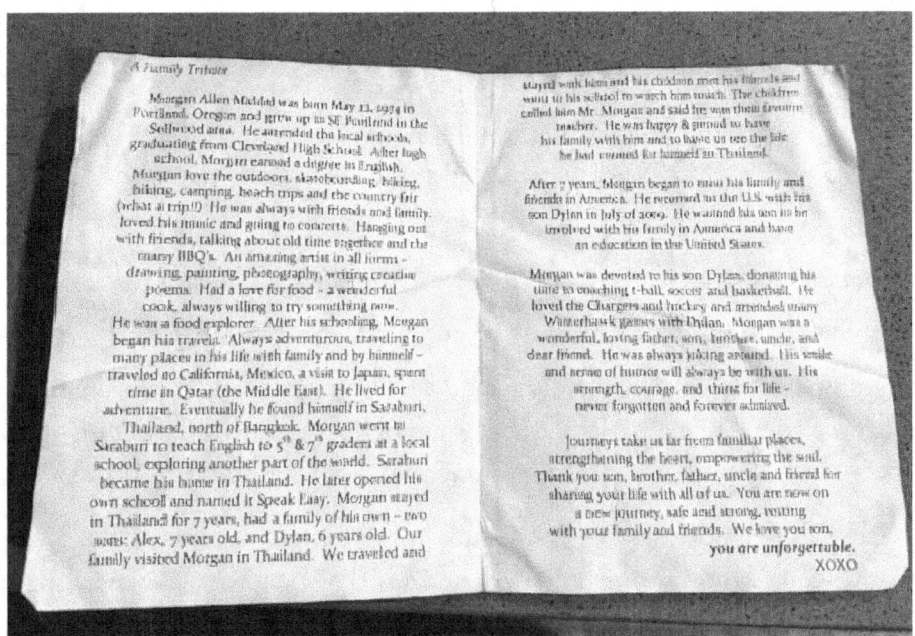

Ko Lipe (Thai: เกาะหลีเป๊ะ, pronounced [kɔʔ lǐːpéʔ]) is a small island in the Adang-Rawi Archipelago of the Strait of Malacca, in Satun Province of southwest Thailand, close to the Malaysian border. Its Thai name, the corrupted form of the original Malay name, Pulau Nipis ('thin island') is transliterated in many different ways into English. The most common names are "Koh Lipe", "Koh Lipeh", "Ko Lipey", and "Ko Lipe".

Lipe Island, also known as Koh Lipe, is a small island in Thailand's southern Andaman Sea, originally inhabited by the "Chao Ley" people, a group of sea gypsies known as the Urak Lawoi, who were granted the island by the Thai government to prevent Malaysian encroachment.

Popular activities for visitors to the island include sightseeing of natural features, water sports such as scuba diving, snorkeling, and kayaking, boat trips to nearby islands and reefs such as Ko Usen and Ko Kra, and drinking and dining, particularly fresh seafood on Walking Street.

Visitors take in sunrise views on Sunrise Beach and partake in nightlife on Pattaya Beach.

Scuba diving and snorkeling around Koh Lipe are often viewed as some of the best in Thailand because of the healthy reefs and range of marine life.

Popular activities for visitors to the island include sightseeing of natural features, water sports such as scuba diving, snorkeling, and kayaking, boat trips to nearby islands and reefs such as Ko Usen and Ko Kra, and drinking and dining, particularly fresh seafood on Walking Street.

Visitors take in sunrise views on Sunrise Beach and partake in nightlife on Pattaya Beach.

Scuba diving and snorkeling around Koh Lipe are often viewed as some of the best in Thailand because of the healthy reefs and range of marine life.

Ko Lipe has three main beaches: Sunset Beach (*Hat Pramong*), Sunrise Beach (*Hat Chao Ley*), and Pattaya Beach. The calm, clear water makes Ko Lipe ideal for snorkeling, with 25 percent of the world's tropical fish species found in the area.

Ko Lipe is also popular with Generation X and typically older generations looking for a peaceful break.

Inclusion: Thailand reminds readers of its diverse and unique aspects, as discussed in the main body of this chapter. It highlights the country's uniqueness, making it stand out from any other place on earth.

Visitors can enjoy sightseeing at elephant farms, visiting temples, and exploring historical landmarks like the ancient city walls in Chiang Mai. Taking a longtail boat ride to different islands in Ao Nang and ending up at Lipe—my favorite island near my hometown—adds to the adventure.

Thailand's rich culture, breathtaking landscapes, and friendly people make it truly special. My grandson, Khai, mentioned how warm and welcoming Thai people are, which makes me consider moving back here with my family. He loves Thailand, and this trip has changed his life.

Thailand is home to significant historical sites such as Ayutthaya, Sukhothai, and Chiang Mai, with their deep-rooted history. While acknowledging Thailand's beauty, it is also important to consider any future challenges and planning aspects depending on one's travel goals and interests.

Mainly, Thailand is a destination that offers a perfect blend of history, culture, natural beauty, and warm hospitality.

Chapter 23

82ⁿᵈ Birthday celebration

Featured Photos ›

Feb 20, 2017   Ju

Media Types ›

▣ Videos		1,493
▣ Selfies		421
◎ Live Photos		10,311
⨍ Portrait		432

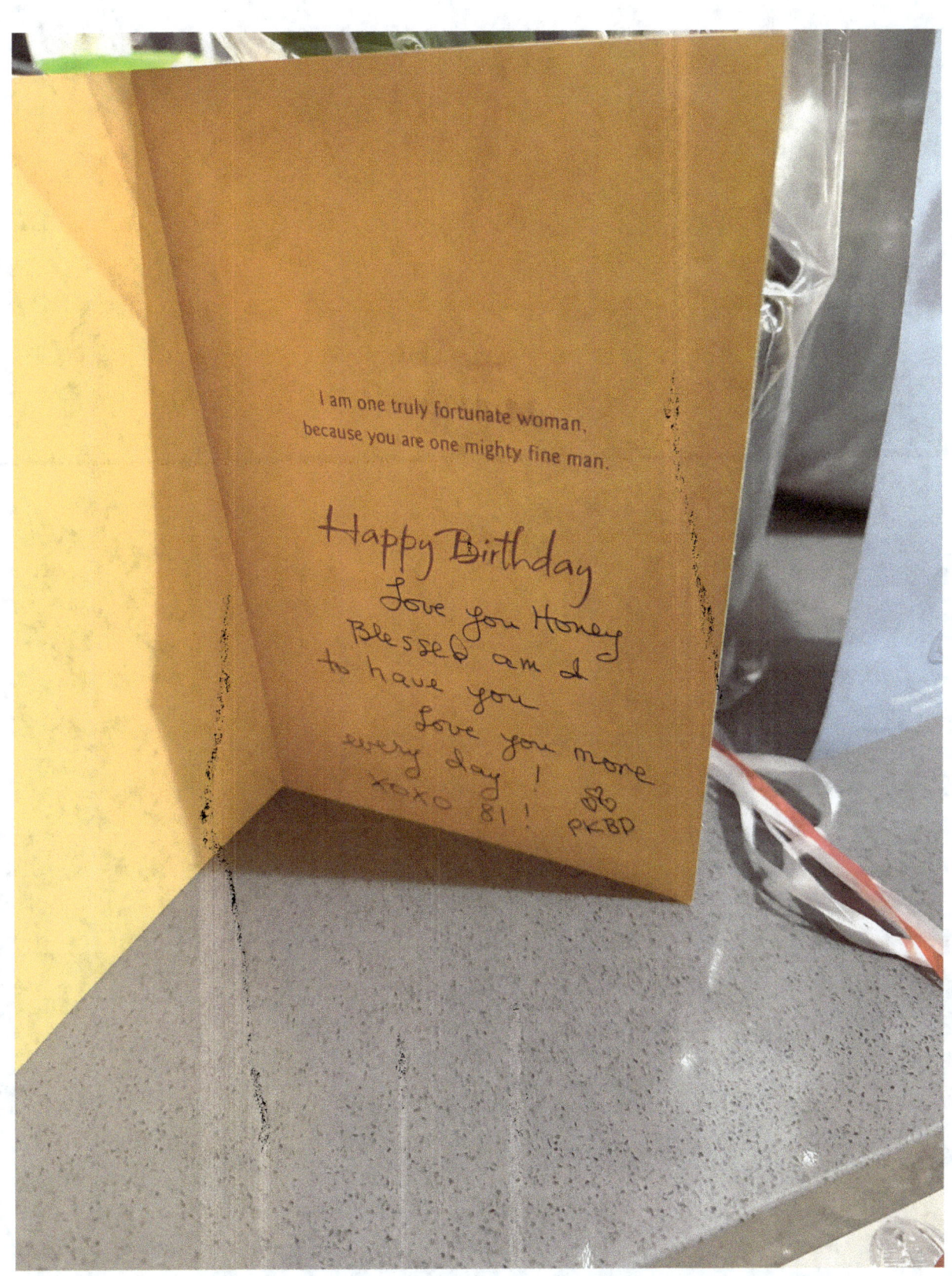

241

 **Dona Dumdeang** is with **Daney Dumdeang**.

10h · 👥

Happy birthday to my Papa. You're truly one of a kind. ❤️

👍❤️ Michele Saris-Middal and 81 others

👍 82   💬 19   🔗   ↪

 **Kimberly Jackson**

As a part of my summer Unitas, my publisher and my assistance requested. I agreed, and I see their points of a significant part of the chapter. Thanks.

I have the greatest opportunity to visit my own country, Thailand in, over 8 years plus after Covid 19, I have not visited my country. So, this trip is quite important to be in-cooperated with my family. My daughter, my son, and my daughter-in-law asked me to make it happen.

First, we had beautifully set up a plan and timetables as well as the group of fifteen people in it. Unfortunately, I had to leave on November 24, 2024, because the Lord took my sister's life to be with him. I changed my plan from leaving on the 12th of December to the 24th of November 2024. It was the hardest decision, but I learned how to manage it for both me and my personal family. I lost my sister and joined with group journey as original planning - as I mentioned in the introduction.

Mainly, Thailand is a destination that offers a perfect blend of history, culture, natural beauty, and warm hospitality.

Thailand has something for everyone, including you, the reader, making it the ideal choice for any traveler,

So pack your bags and embark on a journey to explore the amazing and wonderful land of Thailand. I promise you that it is a truly remarkable and unforgettable destination.

Chapter 24

Celebration of the 77th Birthday of Patty K. Dumdeang

Dr. Danaey Dumdeang's Speech
On the 77th Birthday Party of Patty K. Dumdeang
At The Old Spaghetti Factory Restaurant, Sunday, 4:30 PM, February 23, 2025

Quoted:

"Hello everyone, thank you for coming to this special event—Patty's 77th birthday—for a beautiful girl, sweet lady, my wife, mother, friend, grandma, and everything that she is. She now looks 77—looking great and young. My friend Bob said today in his message:

'Enjoy your drinks, dinner, and ice cream. We will do this again at a happy event like this, okay?'

Happy birthday, my lovely wife. The staff will come and sing the birthday song at the end of this dinner. We will join them.

"Thank you."

Dona Dumdeang   now
To you, Tommy DD & 2 others
iPhone

Today 9:40 AM

Erika

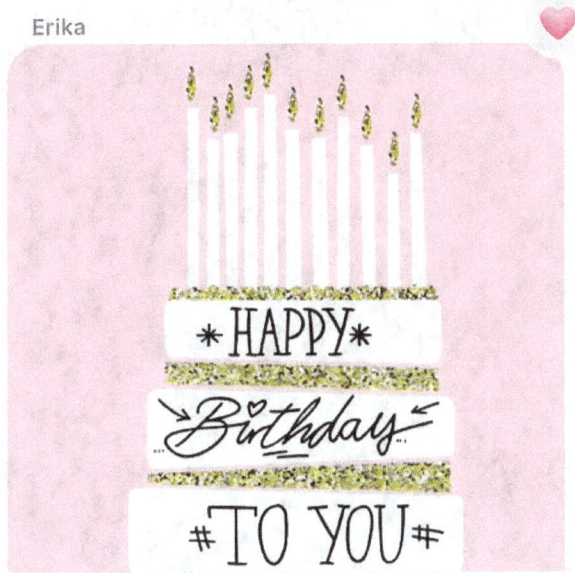

247

248

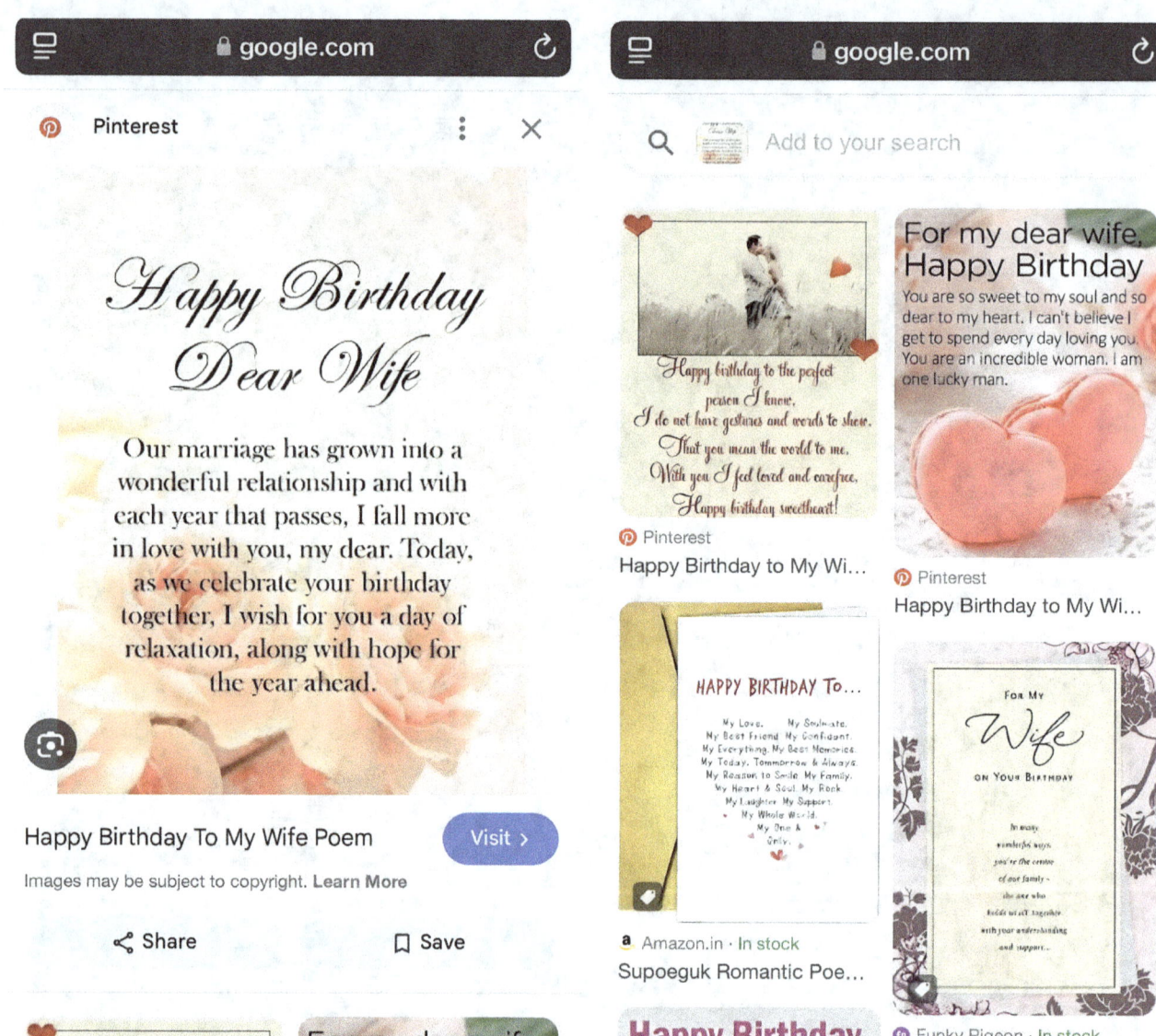

Happy Birthday Dear Wife

Our marriage has grown into a
wonderful relationship and with
each year that passes, I fall more
in love with you, my dear. Today,
as we celebrate your birthday
together, I wish for you a day of
relaxation, along with hope for
the year ahead.

Happy Birthday To My Wife Poem

Visit >

Images may be subject to copyright. Learn More

Share   Save

Pinterest
Happy Birthday to My Wi...

For my dear wife,
Happy Birthday
You are so sweet to my soul and so
dear to my heart. I can't believe I
get to spend every day loving you.
You are an incredible woman. I am
one lucky man.

Pinterest
Happy Birthday to My Wi...

HAPPY BIRTHDAY TO...

Amazon.in · In stock
Supoeguk Romantic Poe...

FOR MY
Wife
ON YOUR BIRTHDAY

Funky Pigeon · In stock
Poem for my Wife Birthd...

Happy Birthday
to my Amazing Wife

Happy Birthday
Dear Wife

Our marriage has grown into a
wonderful relationship and with
each year that passes, I fall more
in love with you, my dear. Today,
as we celebrate your birthday
together, I wish for you a day of
relaxation, along with hope for
the year ahead.

Happy Birthday To My Wife Poem

HAPPY 77 YEAR BIRTHDAY to my
sweet heart. NUMBer means @ 40·4 R still
looking young and beautiful like Bob said
Love unconditionally
your handsome one

02/23/25 Sunday

Ultimate Travel Map and guide of Thailand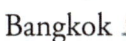

Bangkok 🗼
Grand Palace Wat Pho/Wat Arun
Chatuchak weekend market
Yaowarat (Chinatown)
Train & Floating markets
Erawan Waterfalls tour
Lumphini Park
Khaosan Road

Pattaya City 🏖
Sanctuary of Truth
Wat Phra Yai temple
Nong Nooch Garden
Alcazar Cabaret show
Walking Street

Autthaya
Ayutthaya Historical Park
Visit (many, many temples)

Sukhothai 🍪
Sukhothai Historical Park
(Visit many, many temples)
Si Satchanalai Historical Park
Sukhothai Night Market

Chiang Rai
Wat Rong Khun (white temple)
Wat Rong Suea Ten (blue temple)
Baam Dam Museum (black temple)

Chiang Mai 🐘🐘
Elephant Sanctuary
Wat Doi Suthep temple
Wat Chedi Luang temple
Monk's Trail hike
Sticky Waterfalls
Night Bazaar

Pai 🍄🍄
Pai Canyon
Mo Pang Waterfall
Doi Miang viewpoint (sunset)

Nam Lod cave
Bamboo bridge
Tipsy Tubing

Khao sok 🏞️
Cheow Lan tour (2D/1N)
includes Nam Talu cave,
morning & night safari,
swimming, kayaking & Floating bungalows

Koh Lipe 🏝️
Sunrise & Sunset beach
Koh Adang tour
Koh Usen (kayak/SUP)
Diving spot
Maya Bar/ Corner Bar

Koh Lanta 🏝️
Lanta Animal Welfare
Mu Ko Lanta Park hike
Klong Dao beach
Koh Rok (snorkelling)

Koh Phi Phi 🏝️
Maya Bay tour
Loh Dalum beach
Reggae Bar
Ibiza Pool Party

Koh Tao 🐢
Koh Nang Yuan Island
Diving spot
John-Suwan viewpoint
Sairee Beach / Mango Bay

Koh Samui 🐷
Tarnim Magic Garden
Wat Phra Yai temple
Lamai beach
Koh Mat Sum (Pig Island)

Koh Pha Ngan 🌝 🎉 🍄
Ang Thong Marine Park
Amsterdam Bar (sunset)
Full Moon Party /OXA

Eden Garden / Jungle Ferty

Ao Nang 🏖️ ☂️ 🏖️
4 Islands tour
Railay beach & lagoon
Tiger Cave temple
Rock climbing spot
Night Market

Koh Chang 🐘
Salak Phet Mangrove
Khlong Phlu Waterfall
Jungle trekking

Phuket 🏝️
Phang Nga Bay tour
Wat Chalong temple
Monkey Hill (sunset)
Big Buddha hike
Freedom Beach
Old Town tour
Bangla Road

Hua hin 🏖️ ☂️ 🏖️ 🌊
Cicada Market
Hua Hin Beach
Black Mountain Water Park
Vana Nava Water Jungle
Wat Huay Mongkol
Wat Khao Takiap

Chapter 25

Ubon Dumdeang

Patty,

day is all about

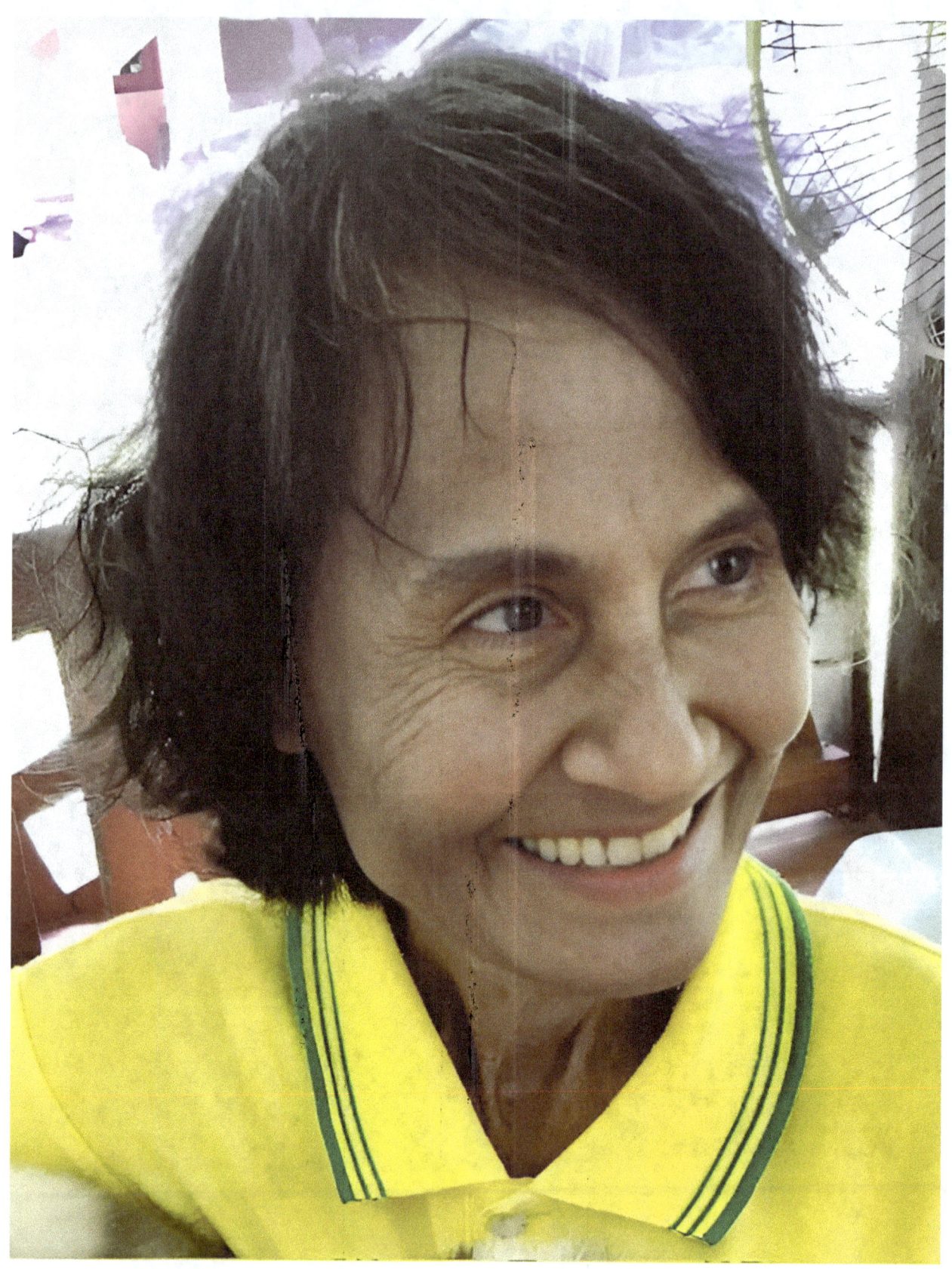

ฌาปนกิจศพ
นางสาวอุบล ดำแดง
(ป้าอุบล)
ชาตะ 15 สิงหาคม 2489
มรณะ 24 พฤศจิกายน 2567

ขอบคุณมากๆจะหลานรัก
0:26 PM

Fri, 11/29

W≡ **คำกล่าวไว้อา...น้องอุบล.docx**
Valid till: 12/6, 02:04
Size: 19.74 kB

Read
2:54 AM

Sat, 11/30

12:04 PM

Sun, 12/1

ดีใจที่ได้พบหลานๆ รักห่วง
Read
4:40 AM

Yesterday

Unread messages below

https://www.facebook.com/
share/r/17GKJFqyK8/?
mibextid=D5vuiz
8:10 PM

พี่ลูกหมีก็ส่งเงินมาให้ป้าทุกเดือน
ส่วนพี่หมอก็จะซื้อนุ่นนี่นั่นมาให้ ให้เงินป้าทุกปี
เสื้อสีเหลืองที่พี่หมอซื้อมาให้ ป้าก็ใส่อยู่นั่นแหละ
ป้าจะชอบมาเล่าให้เราฟังว่าหลานคนนั้นคนนี้ซื้อของมาให้
อาหารเสริมกินแล้วดีแบบนั้นแบบนี้
เพราะในช่วงหลายปีมานี้เราใกล้ชิดกับป้ามากที่สุด
ส่วนป้าสะใภ้ชอบทำกับข้าวมาให้ป้าเอาแกงมาให้
ส่วนแม่ชอบซื้อของที่ป้าชอบมาให้เสมอๆ

ในส่วนของเราคือคนที่รับไม้ต่อจากเจ๊เจ๊
โชคดีได้พาป้าไปหาหมอที่ มอ. ตั้งแต่สมัยนั่งรถประจำทาง
จนขับรถเองได้ ก็ขับพาไปเอง ไปรพจังหวัด เราก็พาไป
โชคดีมีแม่ ไปเป็นเพื่อน
บ้างรอบก็จะเป็นป้าสะใภ้กับน้าหมวย ที่พาไป แต่ถ้ารพ
ประจำอำเภอเราจะพาไปเอง เดินเอกสารให้เอง
ถ้าอยากรู้อาการป้าว่าหมอว่ายังไงบ้าง ต้องมาถามเรา
ตอนป้าไม่สบายเราก็ไปเฝ้า
บางวันเราไปส่งและรับป้าสะใภ้เข้าเวร เราก็จะไปนั่งเล่นที่รพ
วันที่ป้ามีอาการชัก
เรากับป้าสะใภ้นั่งรถพยาบาลไปส่งป้าที่รพจังหวัด

ในชีวิตนี้ไม่เคยสัญญาอะไรกับป้าเลย
แต่ตอนเราอยู่หน้าห้องผู้ป่วยกึ่งวิกฤตที่รพจังหวัด เรา
สัญญากับป้าว่า เราจะอยู่ตรงนี้ไม่ไปไหน
และใช่ว่านาทีที่ป้าช็อกเราอยู่ตรงนั้นคนเดียว
ตอนนั้นประมาณตีห้ากว่า พยาบาลถามหาญาติผู้ป่วย
เราสะดุ้งตื่น ตื่นมาพร้อมกับคำถามที่ว่า คนไข้มีอาการช็อก
ปั๊มหัวใจไหม โชคดีโทรหาแม่ติด แม่นั่งรถไฟขาล่องใต้พอดี
หลังจากที่ไปรักษาตัวแล้วไปอยู่บ้านที่ตจว
ประมาณเกือบสองเดือนเห็นจะได้
แล้วก็ได้แม่เป็นคนตัดสินใจในนาที
เราคงรับสภาพไม่ได้ถ้าพยาบาลถามหาญาติป้า
แล้วไม่มีใครปรากฏตัว เราอยู่หน้าห้อง

Rainy Namfhon Wannaporn
1h · 🌐

ป้าจากพวกเราไปแล้ว1เดือน
พวกเรายังไม่ชิน เหมือนมีอะไรบางอย่างหายไปจากชีวิต
ขับรถผ่านหน้าบ้าน เดินผ่านหน้าบ้าน ยังคิดว่าป้ายังอยู่
พอรู้สึกตัวอีกที
เราต้องยอมรับความจริงว่าป้าไม่อยู่แล้วจริงๆ
ถ้าถามว่าพวกเราคิดถึงป้าไหม ตอบได้เลยว่าคิดถึงมาก
ป้าอาจจะคิดว่า ตอนป้าแก่ป้าไม่มีใครเลี้ยง
เพราะป้าไม่มีครอบครัว แต่ป้าคิดผิดมาก
เพราะป้ายังมีหลานที่ป้าเลี้ยงตั้งแต่เด็กๆไม่ว่าจะเป็นพี่ลูกหมี
พี่ลูกแมว เรา
และยังมีพี่ๆน้องๆหลานๆที่อยู่เคียงข้างป้ามาตลอด
ป้าหันมาเมื่อไหร่ก็เจอ พวกเราอยู่ตรงนี้เสมอ

ภาพในความทรงจำของเราคือป้าเป็นครูศูนย์พัฒนาเด็กเล็ก
สอนเด็กมาหลายรุ่นมาก รวมถึงหลานตัวเองด้วย
ตอนเด็กเรานั่งซ้อนท้ายไปศูนย์เด็กกับป้า
แต่ถ้าเป็นรุ่นก่อนก็จะเป็นพี่ลูกหมี พี่ลูกแมว

พี่ลูกแมวเป็นหลานที่ป้ารักมาก
อยู่กับป้าดูแลป้าพอตัวเองมีครอบครัวก็จะมาหาป้าตลอด
ตัดยางที่สวนแถวบ้านได้ก็จะแบ่งครึ่งกับป้าทุกเดือน
มาเยี่ยมทุกครั้งก็ซื้อของมาฝาก แล้วก็ให้เงินตลอด
ซื้อสร้อยคอทองให้บ้างละ อาหารเสริมบ้าง ค่าน้ำมันรถ
ค่ารักษาพยาบาลเจ๊เจ๊ก็เป็นคนออกตลอด
เจ๊เจ๊เพิ่งมาเยี่ยมป้าก่อนป้าจะมีอาการชักสองวันเอง
และเป็นหลานที่ป้าอยากเจอมากที่สุดในวาระสุดท้ายของชีวิ
ต ขนาดเลขที่ป้าให้ เจ๊เจ๊ก็ถูกหวยดุนเดียวทั้งงาน
ป้าก็จะไม่มาเล่าให้เราฟังตลอด

พี่ลูกหมีก็ส่งเงินมาให้ป้าทุกเดือน

Thank you for your kind and heartfelt words. I am truly honored to have the opportunity to support you during this challenging time. Please know that my thoughts and prayers are with you as you mourn the loss of your beloved sister, Ubon. From everything you've shared, it's clear she was a remarkable woman with a generous spirit, touching countless lives through her work with UNESCO and her kindness during difficult times. Her legacy of love and compassion will live on in the hearts of those she impacted, including yours. I can only imagine how painful this must be for you, especially since you shared such a close bond with her. Your grief and the question, "Why me?" are natural in moments like these.

Please remember, it's okay to cry and take all the time you need to heal. I am here for you—professionally, spiritually, and as a friend—whenever you need support or simply someone to listen. I truly believe that our meeting was no coincidence, and I thank God for the connection we share.

May you find peace and comfort in the cherished memories of your sister and in the knowledge that her kindness and love will always be with you.

I hope you had safe flight to Thailand. Let me know if you need anything.

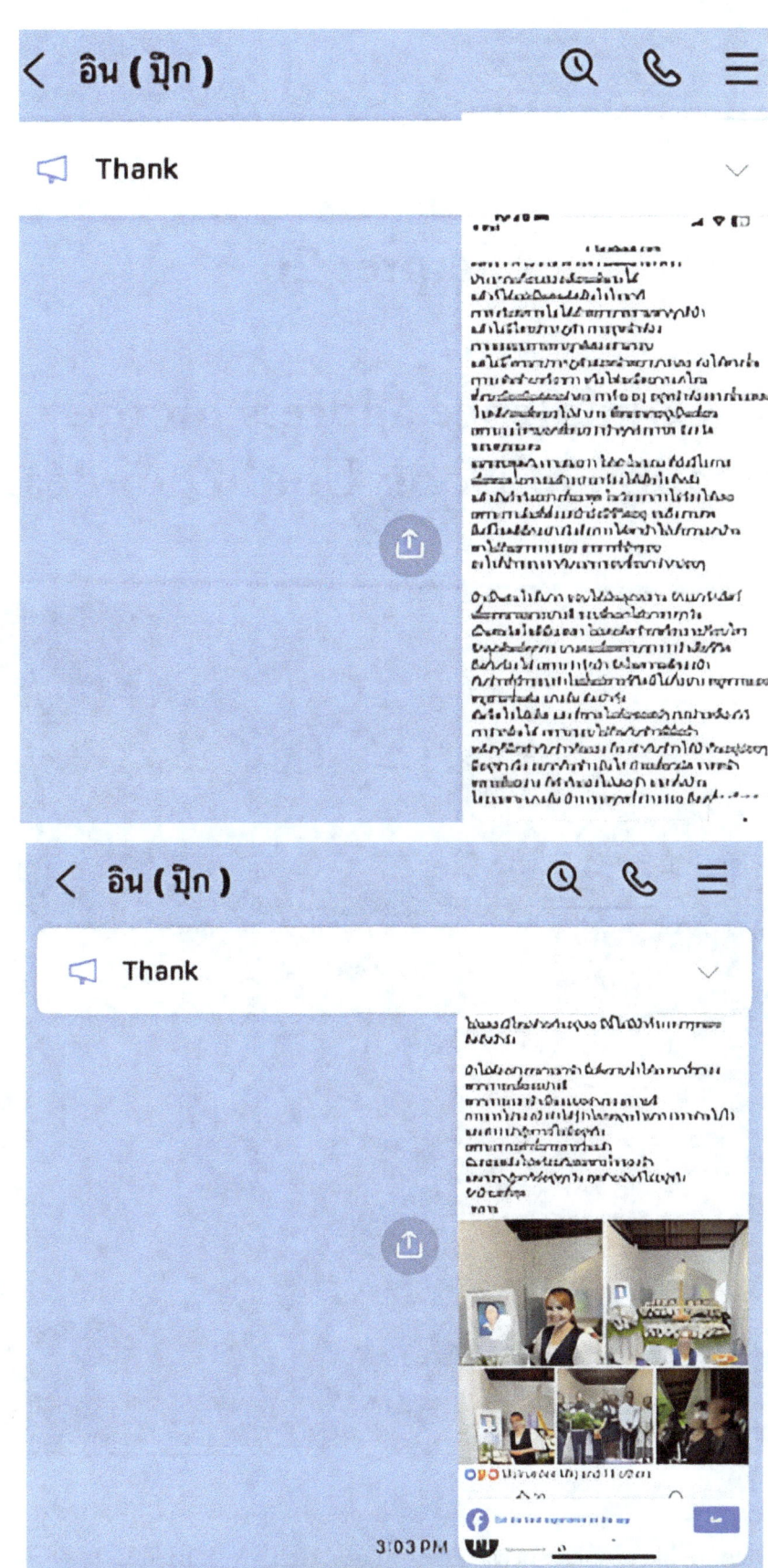

Chapter 26

Condolence address on the cremation of Nong Ubol Dumdeang

Ladies, gentlemen, noble monks, special guests, family, relatives, friends

I'm Dr. Sompong Dumdeang, Ubon's older brother:

Ubon, the fourth child of mother In and father Khai, was born in Baa, Houyang Rankt, Songkhla. She has

- Phi Khin

- Phi Pipat

- Myself (Sompong)

- Nong Ubon

- Nong Jaroon

- Nong Jarun

- Nong Somboon

- Nong Precha

- Nong Piyawan

- Nong Warangkana

Thanks for coming and joining this ceremony for the new life of Ubon and for giving full moral and spiritual support to me and my family.

I have learned that:

All the family gave the best hand to be on duty watching Ubon, days and nights, out of love and concern, trying to save Ubon's life. Drs and medical staff have worked so hard trying to save her life. Furthermore, they agreed with my family to help Ubon to breathe as long as she could.

My schedule was to be here on 12 December with all my family, but after learning from my family here that Ubon had to be in the ICU, I then changed my flight to fly here as soon as I could. This is why the rest of my family from America is not here yet. Thanks to the monks who have been giving spiritual support in the hospital and here in the temple.

From my memory, Ubon has grown with great discipline from our parents' instruction, and she is following the path of family tradition by staying in discipline in the rules and laws of the family. When she was in elementary school at Wat Pangtri School, where I was too, one day, a district officer came to visit our school. The officer asked her to stand up. He pointed her out and said everyone should be dressed beautifully and have hair styled like Ubon. I was so proud of her. And she maintained politeness and a big heart for family and everyone.

I took her to Bangkok to study intensive courses in middle and high school, and along with that, she loved home economy, sewing, and manicure. She worked as a seamstress for a while, then returned home when I left for USA. Later, she worked as a kindergarten teacher. All her students loved her. She was the best at taking care of and being close to our mother. She is the best daughter to a mother; one should look up to her to be like her. She is a good and lovely sister to us; she is a great friend to her friends. She is a great Buddhist laywoman, living her five principles all of her life. She surely is heading to heaven as an angel. She is a great citizen of our country. She is having the best living her lifestyle for herself and society. I'm proud of her. She lived beautifully among us for over seventy-nine years. Ubon said goodbye to us at 2:14 Thai time, my sisters have told me. I was sitting down, meditating, communicating to her in spirit. She is happy in heaven—she is no longer in pain—I am proud of her. She lives her life for others. She is full of love. She lived a simple life like Mother Theresa, here in small community, but her heart so big. We who know should learn how to live life simply so we can live simply, as Mother Theresa said. She touched everyone's heart whom I know. I am proud and honored to be her brother. Next lifetime certainly, we will be brother and sister again, forever and ever, eternally. See you in heaven, my lovely and most beautiful sister. All of family in America sent their love to you. They are here with love and spirits with you. Go happy, ok. Do not worry about your love pets. They will be well taken care of. You have done perfectly on earth. You have done what you have to be done. You are the best sister, best daughter, best in family, best friend, best of the of you heart full of to everyone. Go well, my dear sister. Do not worry about anything left behind. All will be taken care of. My turn to do it for you, never late, and will do well for in all your wishes.

We are here to celebrate her new life. I love the Christian faith to say like this:

DO NOT STAND AT MY GRAVE AND WEEP

Do not stand at my grave and weep

I am not there; I do not sleep.

I am a thousand winds that blow,

I am the diamond glints on snow.

I am the sunlight on ripened grain,

I am the gentle autumn rain.

When you awaken in the morning's hush

I am the swift uplifting rush

Of quiet birds in circled flight.

I am the soft stars that shine at night.. I did not die.

Do not stand at my grave and cry;

I am not there. I did not die.

This is the hardest time for us… I am sure most of us have been there and experienced losing a loved one, like we have lost Ubon.

I never thought that she would leave us so early. Our family from the USA organized to come visit her and the family on December 12, but since she was in ICU, I changed my flight and picked one up on Sunday, November 25—from Portland to Canada, then a direct flight to Bangkok, Thailand. Thirteen hours in the air, and two and a half more hours again. I'm really tired; I'm not young anymore. But my heart, my spirit, my morale, and energy from all of you inspire me—and of course, the will and love of Ubon.

Here I am, thankful again for all of your moral support. How beautiful our Thai culture is. I love it.

Realistically, I'm realizing life as the Buddha teaches us: life is changing, being born, decaying, and passing away. Life is painful. We again live through it, against it, making pain, covering it up, searching for happiness away from dukkha. And the end of life is no-self, *anatta*. We are all living on earth only temporarily and then go to heaven to live life with happiness and permanence through the good deeds we've done—just as Ubon has done for herself and for us.

Ubon has practiced the Four Brahmaviharas all her life. She did better than me. She loved her family, taking care of her nieces and nephews like her own children taking care of our mom as best as she could. She is full of love. She loved everyone she knew.

She practiced *metta, karuna, mudita,* and *upekkha* perfectly—not only for mankind but for animals. She loved cats and dogs like her family. She loved and enjoyed taking care of them. She has many cats and dogs left behind. If you're thinking of Ubon, you can support her cats and dogs that are now without a caretaker since Ubon is gone.

I'm willing to continue to support her cats and dogs as I always have. Her pets are her life. I have a foundation from my dog and cat named Marly Foundation. Marly Foundation has donated to animals around the world, including helping a hero who rescued flood victims in Chiang Rai and passed away. Marly Foundation has contributed to victims and will continue to help support Ubon's pets.

I hope her spirit knows and is happy. We learn from Ubon how to love and respect pets not as mere animals but beyond that—how Ubon loved and enjoyed her pets. Even King Rama IX tried to set an example for us in how to care for animals—dogs, cats, cows, and all pets. They have a life to live, like us.

All the Dumdeangs love pets and give them special care as family—not only as playmates but as companions. That is Ubon. So we may well learn to love pets more like Ubon, making our country full of love and more civilized, like the Western world.

It is time to show that we are the best at giving love, warmth, and help to pets. Ubon has left a living legacy. She is happy in heaven.

See you, my dearest sister, in heaven.

"ปิยโก ขายเต โสโก."

Sadness happens because of love, and I love my sister too much.

I'm sad that she's gone unexpectedly, so I would have so many words to say…

Besides, I have to thank all guests and everyone who attended—your moral, financial, and spiritual support is appreciated. The Dumdeang family thanks everyone.

To lose someone you love is never, ever easy. I'm so happy with our celebrations. My younger sister Ubon's service has been so well done.

Thank you to the cooks, master of ceremonies, monks, and everyone who has supported us.

Anything we have done that may be mistaken or not well received—please accept our apology. Otherwise, I feel amazing. I feel happy seeing those who showed love to my sister.

I love our Thai culture—the way we help and support each other in times like this. It's something hardly seen in other countries, even in America.

We've done it.

Thank you.

Nothing is certain in life.
If you are big, you can be small.
If you are rich, you can be poor.
If you are strong, you can be sick.
(Life, impermanence)

Impermanence, all things are impermanent
Cannot be avoided, diverted, or swayed away
Death comes to both men and women
Death, puts it in everyone

When the time comes, what is left is good and bad
That the person has done everywhere
Therefore, I would like to warn all human beings, all lives
Make yourself have goodness before it is too late
Hold on to the words of the Lord, let's break away
Don't be carried away, develop ego, and be deceived
If we worship the Triple Gem
When we make a decision, we will find the heaven
If we miss, Nirvana, the immortal land
We will probably be in heaven, happily

Missing heaven, being a human, the most blissful
We will definitely not meet the world
(Samanera Wongthon Thimklip)

(Life, impermanence)

Impermanence, all things are impermanent
Cannot be avoided, diverted, or swayed away
Death comes to both men and women
Death, puts it in everyone

When the time comes, what is left is good and bad
that the person has done everywhere
Therefore, I would like to warn all human beings, all lives
Make yourself have goodness before it is too late
Hold on to the words of the Lord, let's break away
Don't be carried away, have conceit, or be deceived
If we worship the Triple Gem
When we make a decision, we will find the heavenly realm
If we miss the heaven, we will be a human being, the ultimate happiness
We will not meet the world, for sure
(Samanera Wongthon Thimklip)

Be mindful, remember, and remember the Dharma, the teachings of the Buddha. The summary is:
1. Four people carry, meaning the four elements of earth, water, wind, and fire
2. Three people parade, meaning impermanence Suffering, Anatta
3. One person sits on a mat, that is the mind
4. Two people take you away, that is, sin, merit
When still alive, chaos, endless
When dead, dying, lying still
The cycle of existence, clearly seen, all true
All things are impermanent, not permanent

Wealth, revolving, changing owners
The body must be separated, irresistible
Born, then extinguished, gone, never to return

Let's wake up quickly from delusion, worldly suffering

Create merit, accumulate merit
Even if born, how many lifetimes, it will be glorious
Happiness, smooth, complete, multiply
Because doing good, supporting, being capital

If you look at a corpse, you will see a corpse
The mind is calm, the corpse is the Dhamma, leading to truth
The corpse teaches us to know, reduce, stop and abandon
Determination is the self, being obsessed with vices

In the future, we will be like this
Not constant, moving, waiting to disappear
Do good, have morality, before dying
Even if you die, you will not regret being a human being

Your elder brother,

Dr.Sompong Daney Dumdeang,

President,

(Dumdeang Foundation,)

933 S.E.Reynolds Street,

Portland, Oregon, 97202,

USA.

Email:dumdeangrealty@msn.com

ปีใหม่ปีที่แล้วพี่หนึ่งกับพวกเรายังพาป้าไปกินข้าวด้วยกัน
ไปฉลองปีใหม่ด้วยกันอยู่เลย ปีนี้ไม่มีป้าก็จะเหงาๆหน่อย
คิดถึงป้าจัง

ป้าไม่ต้องห่วงหมาแมวน้า นี่เพิ่งอาบน้ำให้มะหมาสี่ขาเอง
พวกเราจะเลี้ยงอย่างดี
พวกเราจะเอาป้าเป็นแบบอย่างของความดี
การจากไปของป้าทำให้รู้ว่าโลกหมุนเร็วมาก เวลาผ่านไปไว
และคำว่าปาฏิหาริย์ไม่มีอยู่จริง
เพราะเรารอคำนี้มาหลายวันแล้ว
นับถอยหลังไปพร้อมกับลมหายใจของป้า
และรอปาฏิหาริย์อยู่ทุกวัน สุดท้ายมันก็ไม่อยู่จริง
รักป้าบลที่สุด
  หลาน

😆😢😮 Molruedee Mkj and 19 others

Photos

Memories >

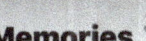

Around the Table
with Sompong
Dumdeang

OVER THE YEARS

Trips >

ทลงจากกาพ เบวรกษ เตวแส ง เบยยม กนทตข ง
ประมาณเกือบสองเดือนเห็นจะได้
แล้วก็ได้แม่เป็นคนตัดสินใจในนาที
เราคงรับสภาพไม่ได้ถ้าพยาบาลถามหาญาติป้า
แล้วไม่มีใครปรากฏตัว เราอยู่หน้าห้อง
เราเจอแบบถามหาญาติสองสามรอบ
แต่ไม่มีใครมาปรากฏตัวต่อหน้าพยาบาลเลย ต่อให้ตรงนั้น
เราจะหันซ้ายหรือขวา หรือไฟจะมืดมากแค่ไหน
ทั้งระเบียงมีแค่คนห้าคน เราก็จะอยู่ อยู่หน้าห้องตรงนั้นแหละ
โชคดีก่อนพี่หมอไปทำงาน พี่หมอมาอยู่เป็นเพื่อน
เพราะแม่โทรบอกพี่หมอว่าป้าถูกส่งมารพ จังหวัด
ขอบคุณนะคะ
แม่ชอบพูดกับเราเสมอว่า ให้ทำในขณะที่ยังมีโอกาส
เมื่อหมดโอกาสแล้วอย่ามาร้องไห้เสียใจทีหลัง
แล้วมันก็จริงอย่างที่แม่พูด ในวันเผาเราไม่ร้องไห้เลย
เพราะเราเต็มที่ตั้งแต่ป้ายังมีชีวิตอยู่ จนถึงงานศพ
สิ่งที่โชคดีอีกอย่างนึงคือการได้พาป้าไปเที่ยวนอกบ้าน
พาไปกินอาหารอร่อย อาหารที่ป้าชอบ
อะไรที่ป้าชอบเรากับแม่จะชอบซื้อมาฝากบ่อยๆ

ป้าเป็นคนใจดีมาก ชอบให้เงินลูกหลาน รักแมวรักสัตว์
เลี้ยงหมาแมวอย่างดี ชอบตื่นมาใส่บาตรทุกวัน
เป็นคนจิตใจดีมีเมตตา ไม่เคยคิดร้ายหรือเอาเปรียบใคร
รักลูกศิษย์ทุกคน บางคนเมื่อทราบข่าวว่าป้าเสียชีวิต
ถึงกับร้องไห้ เพราะว่ารักป้า รักในความดีของป้า
กับข้าวที่ป้าชอบทำในบั้นปลายชีวิตมีไม่กี่อย่าง หมูหวานเอย
หมูสามชั้นต้ม แกงส้ม ต้มยำกุ้ง
ต้มจืดไข่ใส่เห็ด และที่ขาดไม่คือซอสปรุงรสฝาเหลือง55
เราจำกลิ่นได้ เพราะชอบไปกินกับข้าวฝีมือป้า
หลังๆก็ฝึกทำกับข้าวกินเอง ก็จะทำกับข้าวให้ป้ากินอยู่บ่อยๆ
มีอยู่ช่วงนึง อยากกินข้าวมันไก่ ก๋วยเตี๋ยวผัด ราดหน้า
หลายสิ่งอย่าง ก็ทำกินเองไปเลยจ้า แจกทั้งบ้าน
โดยเฉพาะแกงส้ม ป้าจะชมทุกครั้งว่าอร่อย ถึงเครื่องถึงรส

280

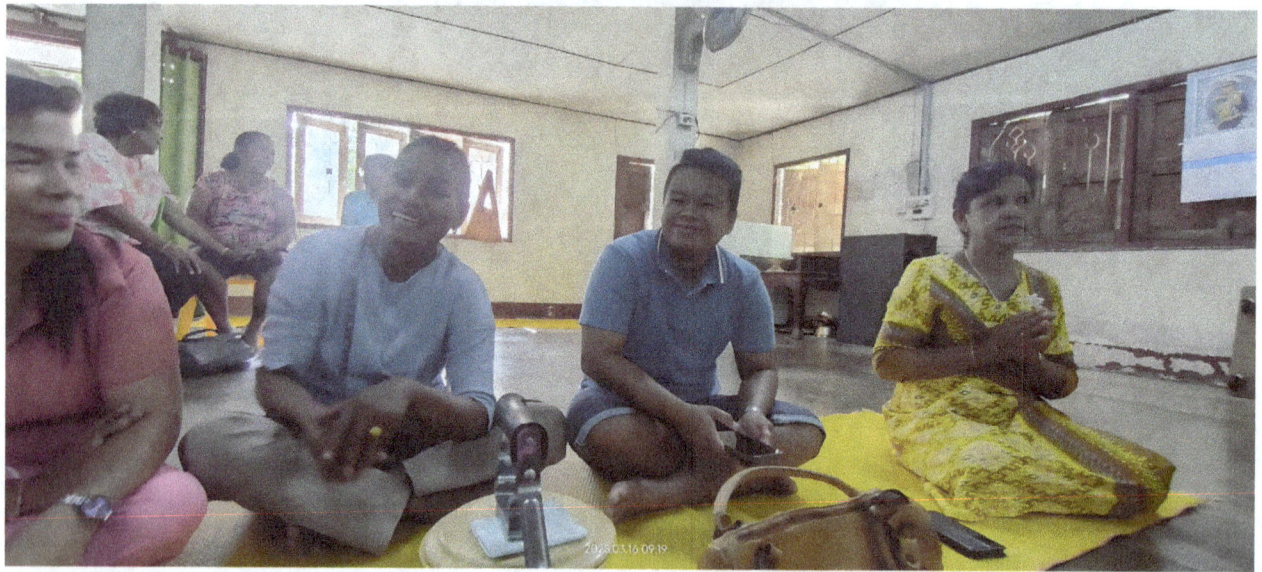

See you again, my lovely sister. If there is a next life, let us be born as siblings in every lifetime.

From your brother

Dr. Sompong Damdaeng

Chairman of the Damdaeng Foundation (Dumdeang Foundation)

933 S.E.Renolds Street, Portland, Oregon, 97202, USA.

Nong Sommai is honest

I intend to publish this book as a tribute to everyone who has contributed to shaping the new life of Sommai Suesattaya.

Thank Note:

The author thanks and thanks Khun Thong Intr Rodpradit, who has assisted in getting this crucial book done in no time. One should recognize his sincere work hard on this book.

Thanks

Dr.Daney.

www.ingramcontent.com/pod-product-compliance
Lightning Source LLC
Chambersburg PA
CBHW081529120626
46550CB00009B/2664